"Harlow has written an original, eminently readable, and thoughtful book on pioneer digital-native news in Latin America, packed with theoretical insights and nuanced arguments. The book examines the rise of these sites amid the disruptions in the news industry in the region, and convincingly demonstrates that they represent a disruptive model that does not fit into traditional categories of mainstream and alternative journalism. With remarkable analytical panache, Harlow helps us to understand how and why innovations happen in sclerotic news ecologies, where journalists and news organizations usually pay a high price for seeking independence and taking risks. The book is a must-read for anyone interested in how positive change in news industries and journalistic practice is possible."

Silvio R. Waisbord, *Director and Professor in the School of Media and Public Affairs at George Washington University, USA*

"This terrific book chronicles the rise of independent, digital-native news sites in Latin America that are inventing a new kind of justice-centered journalism. Harlow makes a strong case for rethinking how and why we classify news outlets as mainstream, alternative, or even hybrid. Her multi-method and multi-perspectival study offers a fascinating look at the "super pioneers"—many of them women—whose innovative approaches to reporting and funding hold promise for rebuilding public confidence in news."

Jennifer Rauch, *Professor and Chair of Journalism & Media Studies at Linfield University Oregon, USA*

Digital-Native News and the Remaking of Latin American Mainstream and Alternative Journalism

Digital-Native News and the Remaking of Latin American Mainstream and Alternative Journalism explores the rise of independent, digital-native news outlets in Latin America and their role in social change, protest participation, and the refinement of the concept of "alternative" media.

Drawing upon a decade of original research, including interviews, surveys, focus groups, and content analyses, this book questions how the emergence of online-native news sites in Latin America is redefining our understanding of what it means to be mainstream and what it means to be alternative. By analyzing a wide range of elements, from business models and audience behaviors to social media use and the role of gender, this text examines how these sites are challenging traditional, hegemonic mainstream news media and its service to political and economic elites. The result is a discerning investigation into the new brand of journalism these sites have innovated.

This insightful study will be of interest to journalism, communication, and Latin American scholars, particularly those interested in how technology is moulding journalistic practices and changing conceptions of journalism itself.

Summer Harlow is an Associate Professor at Jack J. Valenti School of Communication, University of Houston, USA.

Disruptions: Studies in Digital Journalism
Series editor: Bob Franklin

Disruptions refers to the radical changes provoked by the affordances of digital technologies that occur at a pace and on a scale that disrupts settled understandings and traditional ways of creating value, interacting and communicating both socially and professionally. The consequences for digital journalism involve far-reaching changes to business models, professional practices, roles, ethics, products, and even challenges to the accepted definitions and understandings of journalism. For Digital Journalism Studies, the field of academic inquiry which explores and examines digital journalism, disruption results in paradigmatic and tectonic shifts in scholarly concerns. It prompts reconsideration of research methods, theoretical analyses, and responses (oppositional and consensual) to such changes, which have been described as being akin to "a moment of mind-blowing uncertainty."

Routledge's book series, *Disruptions: Studies in Digital Journalism*, seeks to capture, examine, and analyze these moments of exciting and explosive professional and scholarly innovation which characterize developments in the day-to-day practice of journalism in an age of digital media, and which are articulated in the newly emerging academic discipline of Digital Journalism Studies.

Arab Digital Journalism
Noha Mellor

News Journalism and Twitter
Disruption, Adaption and Normalisation
Chrysi Dagoula

For more information about this series, please visit: www.routledge.com/Disruptions/book-series/DISRUPTDIGJOUR

Digital-Native News and the Remaking of Latin American Mainstream and Alternative Journalism

Summer Harlow

LONDON AND NEW YORK

First published 2023
by Routledge
4 Park Square, Milton Park, Abingdon, Oxon OX14 4RN

and by Routledge
605 Third Avenue, New York, NY 10158

Routledge is an imprint of the Taylor & Francis Group, an informa business

© 2023 Summer Harlow

The right of Summer Harlow to be identified as author of this work has been asserted in accordance with sections 77 and 78 of the Copyright, Designs and Patents Act 1988.

All rights reserved. No part of this book may be reprinted or reproduced or utilised in any form or by any electronic, mechanical, or other means, now known or hereafter invented, including photocopying and recording, or in any information storage or retrieval system, without permission in writing from the publishers.

Trademark notice: Product or corporate names may be trademarks or registered trademarks, and are used only for identification and explanation without intent to infringe.

British Library Cataloguing-in-Publication Data
A catalogue record for this book is available from the British Library

ISBN: 978-0-367-71539-7 (hbk)
ISBN: 978-0-367-71534-2 (pbk)
ISBN: 978-1-003-15247-7 (ebk)

DOI: 10.4324/9781003152477

Typeset in Times New Roman
by MPS Limited, Dehradun

This book is dedicated to my beloved mom, Rebecca Harlow, who is dearly missed. Her love of writing, speaking Spanish, and learning about Latin America continues to inspire and influence me.

Contents

List of Tables x
List of Figure xi
Acknowledgments xii

1 The Rise of Independent, Digital-Native Sites in Latin America 1

2 Online Journalism's "Super Pioneers": Entrepreneurship, Innovation, and the Case of Mexico 17

3 Social Media: Likes, Comments, Action! 35

4 Journalism with a Feminist Gaze 55

5 Generating a Journalism That Reforms, Transforms 71

6 Portrait of an Active (Alternative) Audience 89

7 (Dis)Articulations and Disruptions 104

References 121
Index 133

Tables

2.1	Differences in perceptions of innovation, by type of outlet where journalists work	22
3.1	Differences in frequency of social media use, by type of outlet where journalists work	39
3.2	Factors predicting journalists' social media use for work	41
3.3	Comparison of Instagram content, by country	48
3.4	Predictors of Instagram interactions	51
6.1	Factors predicting how often readers accessed the digital-native news sites	96
6.2	Correlations of readers' views of the digital-native sites and their preferred media traits	99
6.3	Factors predicting digital-native news sites' readers protest participation	101

Figure

2.1 Comparison of perceptions about freedom to choose stories among journalists at traditional and digital-native outlets   26

Acknowledgments

I am indebted to everyone who helped make this book a reality.

Thank you to my mentors, colleagues, co-authors, and fellow scholars who have supported and inspired me. I have learned so much from their expertise and guidance.

I especially want to thank everyone who took the time to read preliminary drafts of chapters and provide valuable feedback; this book is so much better because of them. In particular, thank you to Dr. Silvio Waisbord of George Washington University for generously offering to read a draft and then for setting aside time during a busy pandemic semester to Zoom with me and talk through ideas; it was an honor. Mil gracias to Dr. Ingrid Bachmann of the Pontificia Catholic University of Chile for reading my chapters and for always being willing to brainstorm with me. Her constant support as a friend, research partner, travel companion, and fellow Diet Dr Pepper drinker is so much appreciated. Thanks also to Dr. Ramón Salaverría of the University of Navarra for providing feedback on a chapter, and for all his previous research on digital-native news that my work is built on. I also am so grateful to Drs. Dustin Harp, Amy Schmitz Weiss, Victor Perdomo-García, Monica Chadha, Lea Hellmueller, Dani Madrid-Morales, Sally Cruikshank, and my former advisor Tom Johnson for reading drafts of different chapters and giving me invaluable input to make improvements. I couldn't have pulled off writing a book in a pandemic without all of their advice and encouragement.

I also am so thankful to chefão Rosental Calmon Alves and the outstanding Knight Center for Journalism in the Americas research team: Amy Schmitz Weiss, Vanessa de Macedo Higgins-Joyce, Lourdes Cueva-Chacón, and Magdalena Saldaña. Their support made this book possible, as much of the survey and focus group raw data in this book comes from Knight Center projects we were all part of.

Thank you, as well, to Bob Franklin, editor extraordinaire, for his patience, and for approaching me to write this book, otherwise I might not have had the courage to do so.

I also want to say thank you to all the journalists who let me interview them over the years. I am especially grateful to everyone, past and present, at *El Faro* for allowing me to spend so much time learning from them, and for always making me feel at home. May their journalism continue to be a beacon for independent journalism everywhere.

Last but certainly not least, I am so thankful to my family and friends, whose unconditional love is behind all of my accomplishments. So much gratitude goes to my partner and husband, Erik Hernandez, and our dog, Piñata, for supporting me through this journey, being understanding of the extra-long work hours, and forgiving any missed walks or backyard playtimes. Thanks also to my dad, Mike Harlow, and aunt, Ginger Lloyd, for their constant encouragement. And I am forever thankful to my mom. She was always my biggest supporter and believed I could do anything. She would have been so proud of me, and the first person to buy this book.

1 The Rise of Independent, Digital-Native Sites in Latin America

In 1998, Salvadoran journalist Carlos Dada and businessman Jorge Simán founded *El Faro* (Spanish for "lighthouse"), which claims to be Latin America's first digital-native newspaper.[1] At the time—three years after the Internet became publicly available in El Salvador—less than 1% of the population had Internet access, the country was still reeling from a bloody war that had ended just six years prior, and there was no real tradition of independent journalism. Dada was a print newspaper journalist, and didn't have some lofty idea about digitizing the news and spearheading Salvadoran journalism's entrée into the online realm. For Dada, the Internet was the cheapest way to pursue the kind of journalism he believed his country needed. "*El Faro* was started to be different," he told me in 2011, as the site was entering its teens. "It wasn't about objectivity, so much as about honesty and openness. It's a different kind of journalism for El Salvador."

A radically "different" kind of journalism is what independent, digital-native news sites like *El Faro* have come to be known for throughout Latin America. In fact, Latin America is at the leading edge of this trend toward remaking journalism. The journalism these sites offer is a far cry from the market-oriented model of traditional, corporate, mainstream media. They proudly proclaim their editorial and financial independence, prioritizing public interest over profits. They rely heavily on foundation funding, making long-term sustainability a perpetual quest, but also allowing these sites to practice critical, independent journalism, offering counter narratives and including voices and perspectives normally ignored by mainstream media.

As outsiders to a media system that favors the political and economic status quo, these sites see themselves as offering an idealized, professional journalism whose responsibilities lie with serving the public interest by defending human rights and democracy. Their critical, often oppositional, stances make them targets for harassment, attacks, and

DOI: 10.4324/9781003152477-1

accusations of ideological bias or partisanship. Most of these sites, though, don't identify as alternative or activist media. Rather, they offer an alternative to the mainstream, working within and against the system to reform it and regenerate a journalism that challenges our understanding of what the region's journalism *should* be. These sites are pioneering new—counter—approaches to financing, narratives, sourcing, social media, audiences, identity, and journalistic norms and values, innovating a different way of thinking about journalism that is disrupting the entire news media landscape. Ultimately, this book illustrates under what circumstances these independent, digital-native sites exhibit articulations both toward and away from alternative and mainstream journalism, contributing to how we understand digital and traditional, as well as mainstream and alternative, media throughout Latin America, with even broader implications for how independent news startups around the world are inventing a new brand of justice-centered journalism that can't be easily explained by conventional categorizations like mainstream, alternative, or even hybrid.

A lighthouse

El Faro is key to understanding this innovative model of independent digital-native media, its place in the region's journalism landscape, and its disruption of the news industry more broadly. Born a decade before Latin America's explosion of digital-native news outlets, *El Faro* has served as a model of independent journalism—a true lighthouse—for many of these sites, which have been referred to as "generators of change" for their innovation in business models and reporting approaches (SembraMedia, 2017). Between 2010 and 2014, the number of such sites in Latin America grew by 73% (Meléndez Yúdico, 2016). At the time of writing, the Observatorio de Nuevos Medios[2] (New Media Observatory) had cataloged 892 digital-native sites in 19 Spanish-speaking countries of Latin America.

When I first visited *El Faro* in the summer of 2011, Dada, his site, and its reporters were gaining prestige and—at least among mainstream media and elite political circles—notoriety. With influence, though, came surveillance and attacks. *El Faro's* journalists still regularly face threats from gangs and the government, and at the time, armed guards stood watch outside the site's office and accompanied journalists when they went out on stories. Elver,[3] who had started at *El Faro* a decade before when he was just 19, boasted that the site's journalists were "a pebble in the shoe that bothers power." *El Faro* reporters also irked their counterparts at traditional media (an unspoken role prohibited the local press from quoting *El Faro*), who sometimes came across as jealous, noting that the *El Faro* reporters thought they were "better than everyone else."

The *El Faro* journalists themselves talked about what they did as "different" and "better"; they saw themselves as the counterweight to political and media power. They came to *El Faro*, they said in interviews, because of its high journalistic standards, the "freedom" and "independence" to cover what they wanted, and because they wanted to make an "impact." A profile written for the *Columbia Journalism Review* noted that *El Faro* had "become one of Latin America's most trusted news sites" (Maslin, 2016). As Raúl, a 40-something journalist told me, he had left one of the country's leading newspapers to take a "risky" job with the then-newly founded *El Faro* because he wanted to "ease his conscience" after years of watching mainstream news content be manipulated to serve elite political and economic interests. Other journalists espoused similar reasons for joining *El Faro*. Omar, 29, explained,

> The role of *El Faro* is very important for El Salvador, and the reason I'm still here is because this newspaper is necessary, because the other media are too partial—they function in favor of power, whether the government or businesses. I'd like to live in a country like the one Carlos Dada imagines—a better, correct country. This is the main reason I'm here.

The journalists were proud to be able to say their work made a difference. As 21-year-old Julia said,

> *El Faro* changes certain things in the country. We have the role of denouncing, which is something no other newspapers do, and the public knows this about us, and the journalists here risk themselves to do this ... No one else is doing good work, good journalism, like this, and when we do, it's noted.

Journalists repeatedly referred to *El Faro* as "independent," distinguishing themselves from traditional, corporate media. Financial autonomy, lack of ideological affinities to political parties or religion, counter-hegemonic narratives, and opposition to media corporations have all been identified as aspects of what it means to be "independent" in Latin America (Carvalho & Bronosky, 2017; Rovai, 2018). These digital-native sites' independence has become a battle cry, at once providing them with a unique identity, and justifying their criticism of traditional outlets that, whether through cooptation, harassment, intimidation, or violence, have been "captured" by elites (Segura & Waisbord, 2016).

In a region with high levels of media concentration, and in a country where just a few elite families own most of the media outlets and have ties to other major industries, *El Faro's* claim to financial and editorial independence is striking. Its journalists aren't deterred by advertiser or public backlash, or fear of angering ruling authorities, police, or political elites. Their insistence on "complicating the moral landscape" (Maslin, 2016) by reporting on violence—such as a truce between the president's administration and gangs, or human rights abuses by police and jails against gang members—often leads to accusations that the site defends and protects gang members. They've even been accused of being gang members themselves, or laundering money for gangs. In one of the most dangerous countries in the Western hemisphere, where gangs are blamed for much of the violence, *El Faro's* dedication to covering not just violence but its roots—the site in 2011 launched Sala Negra, or Black Chamber, to investigate violence—has pushed reporters beyond merely "describing" what happened, to "denouncing" it (Maslin, 2016). Such counternarratives are fundamental to the site's distinct identity as independent and different than traditional media.

Independent, digital-native media

Digital media throughout Iberoamerica have transformed from being secondary players in the media field to being recognized as key to journalism now, and in the future (Salaverría, 2016). In some countries, like the Dominican Republic and Nicaragua, these media represent their country's first form of online journalism (Salaverría, 2016). And, like *El Faro*, these outlets started online out of economic necessity. While many envisioned having a print version eventually, few (like the Dominican Republic's now defunct *Clave Digital*) actually achieved it.

Despite being online-only outlets in countries with stark digital inequalities, these Latin American sites have garnered success and influence (Harlow & Salaverría, 2016). Looking at influence and reach is important to understand what kind of impact online-only sites can have in a region where 32% of the population lacks Internet access (IADB, 2020). Considering, though, the international prizes and esteem these sites have achieved, and that many are fairly young and still gaining readership, it is technologically deterministic and short-sighted to dismiss these sites' potential effect on the region's journalism. For example,

El Faro, one of the region's winningest digital-native sites, has brought home the most-prestigious international journalism awards: the Gabriel García Márquez prize from the Gabo Foundation, the King of Spain International Journalism Award, and an Ortega y Gasset award; plus, a number of its journalists have won the Maria Moors Cabot Prize, administered by the Columbia Journalism School. In his edited book on online journalism in Iberoamerica, Salaverría (2016) listed some of Latin America's most notable digital-native outlets. Ten of these sites joined forces back in June 2013 to form a transnational association, Aliados (Allies), aimed at using technology to promote transparent, independent, and rigorous journalism throughout Latin America, and to cover the region in ways that mainstream media do not (Knight Center, 2013). The Aliados network comprised *Agência Pública* (Brazil), *Animal Político* (Mexico), *Ciper* (Chile), *Confidencial* (Nicaragua), *El Faro* (El Salvador), *El Puercoespín* (Argentina), *IDL-Reporteros* (Peru), *La Silla Vacía* (Colombia), *Plaza Pública* (Guatemala), and *The Clinic* (Chile), which are among the sites included in research for this book.

Underlying this phenomenon of digital-native media is a devotion to editorial independence, manifest in an emboldened journalism that denounces the political status quo and contests a legacy media ecosystem dominated by commercial and political interests. "Some [digital] natives have assumed the flag of independence as a counter-power, almost as a militancy to position issues that are, in their opinion, relevant to the public, but absent or without sufficient coverage in the traditional agenda" (Zuluaga Trujillo & Gómez Montero, 2019, p. 306). In writing about online media in Canada, Beers (2006) defined independent media as "owned, operated, and structured to allow reporting and commentary that compensates for and counters the corporate media consensus" (p. 116). Independence allows these digital-native sites to take ownership of *real* journalism unmanipulated by elites, and guided not by profit, but by purpose. And that purpose goes beyond informing—these sites are innovating a justice-centered journalism, exposing, denouncing, and in many cases, calling for change in political, economic, social, and media systems.

These sites are "challenging the news" (Forde, 2011) by covering topics marginalized by commercial, corporate media (Zuluaga Trujillo & Gómez Montero, 2019), innovating storytelling formats and audience relations (Higgins Joyce & Harlow, 2020; Méndez et al., 2019), and adopting non-traditional business and funding models (Harlow, 2021a; Tejedor et al., 2020). In interviews with digital-native news site directors in Colombia, García-Perdomo and Magaña (2020) found the sites to be "creative laboratories" that provided an "alternative voice to mainstream media content" (p. 3076). It's worth noting, though, that the Colombian journalists in that study didn't explicitly call themselves "alternative." Likewise, the *El Faro* journalists also did not identify as "alternative" journalists, although they readily acknowledged they offered the best alternative to mainstream media. They just didn't want to use that label.

And therein lies the impetus for this book. Scholars have long debated what makes alternative media "alternative," and the emergence of digital technologies and far-right extremist sites have further complicated our understanding of alternative media. In particular, the rise of independent, digital-native news sites in Latin America—one of the most significant transformations in the region's journalism—calls into question what makes a news outlet "alternative" or "mainstream." These sites take pride in distinguishing themselves from traditional journalism and yet balk at the "alternative" label. Hundreds of such digital-native news sites have come online throughout the region since the new millennium, providing the opportunity for this book to offer not just an overview of these sites, but also to interrogate how they're disrupting Latin American journalism as they re-position what it means to be mainstream and alternative. This book uses data from interviews,[4] observations, focus groups, surveys with audiences and journalists, and the content journalists produce, ultimately showing how these sites are reforming and transforming journalism, with the potential to serve as blueprints for other news outlets.

As the journalism industry worldwide reckons not just with technological disruptions but also a crisis of public confidence and growing distrust among journalists of their industry's status quo, this book offers one possible path forward: independent, digital-native news sites in opposition to traditional ways of doing journalism and (re)generating a journalism of change and resistance. It's a *sui generis* model of journalism that, while foregrounded in Latin America, has import for journalism studies globally. Consequently, this book maps the tensions and negotiations between these sites' orientations toward mainstream/alternative and professional/activist media to identify how digital-native news sites in Latin America are disrupting our understandings of mainstream *and* alternative journalism, thereby changing the journalism landscape broadly.

Alternative journalism

Scholars and practitioners around the world have conceived of alternative media as a corrective for mainstream media. Whether through product or practices, alternative media have been vaunted for the ways they fulfill needs unmet by mainstream media, amplify marginalized voices, focus on participatory and pluralistic processes and content, and shun corporate ways and commercial funding in favor of horizontal and often non-profit organizational structures (Hájek & Carpentier, 2015).

Despite efforts at classification, a universal definition has eluded scholars, who have designated myriad ways to refer to alternative media: radical, grassroots, citizens' media, participatory, community, popular, autonomous, and so on. Among Latin American research, Festa (1986) identified 33 distinct labels, and nearly 40 years later, considering the field's "complex and multifaceted" nature and that it has always been "rebellious to conceptual formalization" (Vinelli, 2014, p. 38), there's no doubt more could be added.

Rauch (2021) contended that *both* alternative and mainstream media represent ideal-types, and each category sometimes expresses characteristics of the other. Still, despite the blurring of the lines between the two, and despite them being part of the same interdependent hybrid media system, alternative and mainstream media *are* different, particularly when it comes to their motivations, and especially in the minds of producers and consumers. Thus, following Rauch's (2021) approach, I use the terms alternative and mainstream broadly to signify ideal-types.

It is also important to note how all-encompassing the term "alternative" is, capturing everything from blogs and social media to zines, art, and graffiti to legacy and digital news publications. Herein I focus on the subcategory of alternative journalism, or "alternative media practices that involve reporting and/or commenting on factual and/or topical events" (Harcup, 2016, p. 684). Scholars typically locate alternative journalism outside the mainstream—amateurs with little professional journalism training (Atton & Hamilton, 2008) producing content outside the "consensus" of what's "acceptable" (Hirst, 2009). Importantly, alternative journalism is not fixed, but evolves as it reacts to changing contexts. This relational perspective is key to my goal here of identifying digital-native sites' articulations toward and away from alternative and mainstream journalism.

Ameliorating the mainstream

Rucht (2004) suggested protesters and activists respond to the shortcomings of mainstream media in four main ways: *abstention, attack, adaptation,* and *alternatives.* Freedman (2017) added a fifth "A":

amelioration, or efforts to reform mainstream media. As I argue throughout this book, Latin American digital-native news sites have taken on this amelioration role, not just resisting traditional, mainstream media but offering a blueprint for what a reformed journalistic field could look like. The very creation of these sites can be conceived as a form of media activism, or a media movement to reform media policies, structures, and norms surrounding access, diversity of voices, funding, security, and ownership (Bennett, 2017).

The idea that digital-native news sites in Latin America are part of a movement to reform, or ameliorate, traditional, corporate media fits with what Monica Chadha and I found among online-only news startups in India. In interviews with founders of Indian entrepreneurial news sites, we classified these entrepreneurs according to an entrepreneurial identity typology (Fauchart & Gruber, 2011): Darwinians, Communitarians, and Missionaries. Darwinians, focused on being a commercial success, are perhaps most closely aligned with the ideals of mainstream media—commercial interests, profit oriented, and corporate ownership. Communitarians, all about being part of and supporting the community, can be linked to community media tenets, while the Missionary identity, aimed at advancing a social or political cause, parallels the ideals of alternative media. In our interviews, though, we identified the need for a new, fourth journalism-specific identity, which we referred to as *Guardian*. Guardians exhibited characteristics, to varying degrees, of the three other identities—they valued profitability and competition for their connection to sustainability and success, they offered distinct value to the community, and they wanted to make the world better. What made Guardians unique, though, was their desire to generate quality journalism: dissatisfied with mainstream media, these Guardian founders used new technologies to produce a transformed version of journalism. Guardians "saw themselves as safeguards of journalism tasked with re-inventing quality, credible, and sustainable journalism" (Harlow & Chadha, 2019, p. 15). The Guardian identity, with its shifting overlaps with the Darwinian, Communitarian, and Missionary identities, is useful for thinking about how to situate the independent, digital-native Latin American news sites in their amelioration role in relation to alternative and mainstream media.

At the margins

These sites are not clear-cut examples of the ideal-type of alternative *or* mainstream media, but at different times under different circumstances exhibit characteristics of both and neither. Articulation theory thus is useful for understanding these sites' connections and disconnections to the mainstream and alternative. Platon and Deuze (2003) implicitly drew on articulation to position online alternative news in relation to mainstream journalism. Articulation, or the process by which unfixed, unnecessary links are made (Hall, 1986), is "both a way of understanding how ideological elements come, under certain conditions, to cohere together within a discourse, and a way of asking how they do or do not become articulated, at specific conjunctures, to certain political subjects" (Hall, 1986, p. 53). While Platon and Deuze did not discuss this theory outright, they viewed the alternative news site Indymedia as "articulated to (a type of) mainstream journalism" (p. 340) for the way its journalists' discourse about ideology, practice, access, and process intersected differently with alternative and mainstream ideals. Other scholars (Atton, 2003; Harcup, 2013) also have noted the crossover between the two genres, and argued for a hybrid understanding of alternative media that both breaks with and draws from mainstream media.

Using Bourdieu's (1993) concept of field theory, Atton and Hamilton (2008) built on the idea of hybridity to suggest that alternative journalism operates in liminal spaces, between the fields of journalism and activism. Rather than rely solely on "alternative" or "mainstream" to fully explain what these media are or are not, Atton and Hamilton approached the two genres in terms of sub-fields: large-scale, mass production concerned with accruing economic capital, and small-scale production, mostly autonomous from market forces and focused on cultural capital. Much of alternative journalism takes place at the boundaries of the sub-fields:

> What is important here is to posit alternative journalism not only as occupying the sub-field of small-scale production, but to consider it as able to occupy liminal positions: whether at the juncture of the two sub-fields of journalism or between an activist (or other) field and the journalistic field.
> (Atton & Hamilton, 2008, p. 134)

Like alternative journalism, independent, digital-native sites occupy precisely such a liminal space. Understanding these sites as operating from the margins of mainstream *and* alternative journalism allows us to identify the ideal-type traits, values, and practices of each genre that, depending on the circumstances, at times complement or challenge each other, creating various (dis)articulations. These sites thus are differentially oriented, or articulated, toward mainstream and alternative journalism, varying according to which tenet or ideal is under examination. The differing articulations often come at the expense of another. The medium also matters, as different technologies and digital platforms and tools prompt different orientations. Ultimately, I will show how these sites use their articulations toward the mainstream precisely in order to challenge and reform—ameliorate—mainstream media and the journalism field more broadly.

Latin American journalism

Latin America is vast and diverse, comprised of Spanish-, Portuguese-, and Indigenous language-speaking countries in North, Central, and South America and the Caribbean: Argentina, Brazil, Bolivia, Chile, Colombia, Costa Rica, Cuba, the Dominican Republic, Ecuador, El Salvador, Guatemala, Honduras, Mexico, Nicaragua, Panama, Paraguay, Puerto Rico, Peru, Uruguay, and Venezuela. More than 650 million people live in this region, comprising roughly 8% of the world's population. These countries share commonalities and differences in their political, cultural, economic, and media systems, such as governmental corruption, impunity, cyber surveillance, judicial and self-censorship, defamation lawsuits, clientelist corporate media, and lack of media pluralism (RSF, 2021). Research has categorized Latin American media as part of "captured liberalism" (Guerrero & Márquez-Ramírez, 2014), where, despite open competition and a private, commercial model, a concentrated media system has emerged where press freedom and pluralism are constrained by the interests of political and economic elites (Hughes & Lawson, 2005; Rockwell & Janus, 2010). Still, there is no one media system or model applicable to every country (Hanitzsch et al., 2019). Differing journalistic roles, cultures, and even ethics have been identified to various extents throughout Latin America (Higgins Joyce et al., 2017; Mellado et al., 2012).

Reporters Without Borders' 2021 press freedom rankings of 180 countries worldwide range from a regional high of 5 (Costa Rica) to lows of 151 (Honduras) and 171 (Cuba). Considering just a few of the region's specific country contexts at the time of writing gives insight into the common challenges to Latin American journalism. *Argentina's* press freedom score has dropped in recent years in part because of media concentration and judicial harassment and lawsuits against independent journalists. In *Bolivia*, journalists face state censorship, judicial harassment, arbitrary arrests, and financial and physical attacks, all of which contribute to self-censorship. Journalists in *Brazil* are regularly attacked by the president and his supporters, and the country is one of the most dangerous countries for journalists, especially those covering corruption or organized crime. While *Chile* has higher levels of press freedom than most Latin American countries, the media system is highly concentrated, journalists for community and Indigenous media often are at risk, and during recent protests journalists were targeted and attacked. Since 2016, journalists in the *Dominican Republic* can no longer be jailed for defamation, but journalists who cover corruption and drug trafficking still face threats and attacks, and high levels of impunity and media concentration result in self-censorship. In *Ecuador*, journalists critical of the government have been fired, attacked and sued for defamation, and a recent rise in violence increasingly puts journalists at risk. *El Salvador* remains one of the most violent countries in Latin America, putting journalists who cover gangs, drug trafficking, or government corruption at risk, and the president also regularly harasses independent journalists. *Guatemala* also is one of the Western hemisphere's most dangerous countries for journalists, with low levels of press freedom related to physical violence against and killings of journalists, self-censorship, organized crime, impunity, and high media concentration. In *Honduras*, media freedom has steadily declined since the 2009 coup, and police and military regularly attack and threaten journalists, who also face defamation lawsuits and even outright bans on journalism. *Mexico* is one of the world's most dangerous countries for journalists because of organized crime, government corruption, and a weak judicial system. Independent journalists in *Nicaragua* are in a media war started by the president, and they regularly endure official harassment, arrests, and threats. In *Peru*, journalists, especially those covering environmental conflicts, corruption, and drug trafficking, are hampered by defamation lawsuits. Despite some cases of threats, political pressure, and judicial harassment, *Uruguay* has one of the world's highest levels of press freedom and is seen as a regional model for its laws favoring information access and media pluralism. In *Venezuela*, where most print outlets have shuttered and critical radio and TV stations been kicked off the air, the state controls most media and the government tries to silence independent journalists via threats, violence, and arbitrary arrests. Finally, in *Cuba*, the Latin American country with the worst press-freedom ranking, the government maintains control over the media, and independent journalists and bloggers are regularly surveilled, subject to home searches and equipment confiscation, and arbitrarily arrested.

Despite some country differences, this book adopts Segura and Waisbord's (2016) understanding of the region's media systems as comprising a "common Latin American model" dominated by "the market and politics rather than the demands and expectations of multiple publics" (pp. 15–16). Such a limited pluralism model has resulted in the concentration of media ownership and the creation of media oligopolies, where a handful of companies, often led by powerful families, control the bulk of broadcast licenses, newspapers, and advertising. These media companies also are typically owned by groups that have their hand in other important economic sectors, like agriculture, banking, and retail (Becerra & Mastrini, 2010; Rockwell, 2017). These oligopolies are further strengthened by a weak public media model, the marginalization of alternative and community media, and media clientelism, or the quid-pro-quo relationships between media companies and political and economic elites (Segura & Waisbord, 2016). The result of such "elite-captured media," as Segura and Waisbord (p. 31) termed it, is that "homogeneity rules over diversity in content and cultural forms" (Sandoval-García, 2008, p. 100).

Latin America's media remain understudied compared with the rest of the world (Salaverría & de Lima-Santos, 2021), allowing this book to further sharpen the picture of journalism in the region. In looking at 25 years of research on digital journalism globally, Salaverría (2019) identified five aspects fundamental to the development of online journalism in coming years: the role of women, financial sustainability, more technological training, market-oriented production, and participation/collaboration. As I will show throughout this book, digital-native media in Latin America already have begun taking on these challenges—their innovation with business models, counternarratives, values, norms, practices, audience relations, and technology make these outlets key to understanding the ongoing evolution of Latin America's journalism, and the distinct journalistic identity these sites have pioneered.

Book outline

This book is based on a decade of qualitative and quantitative research I've conducted on independent, digital-native news sites in Latin America. This research includes in-depth interviews with journalists and activists, focus groups with journalists and news site founders, surveys of audiences and journalists, and textual and content analyses of stories and social media posts from digital-native news sites, as well as mainstream media. The survey and focus group data presented here come from research I conducted with the Knight Center for Journalism in the Americas at the University of Texas at Austin. The Knight Center's research team has produced important work—about the nature of these news sites, their funding, their innovation, and their impact on journalism education and newsroom practices—that helped inspire this book (Cueva Chacón & Saldaña, 2021; Higgins Joyce et al., 2017; Saldaña et al., 2017; Schmitz Weiss et al., 2017, 2018, 2020).

Having laid out an introduction to alternative media and this booming trend of digital-native media in Latin America, let me offer a brief outline of the chapters to come. Chapter 2 explores how independent, digital-native news startups in Latin America are pioneering new approaches to financial and editorial independence. Innovation and sustainability are interwoven with how journalists perceive and lay claim to quality journalism. Additionally, this chapter takes a deep dive into the proliferation of independent, online-native sites in Mexico. In a country beset by government corruption and violence, the case study sheds light on the ways these sites perceive violence as an entrepreneurial opportunity representing an opening for journalistic and social change via innovation in financial and editorial independence.

In Chapter 3, I examine the challenges and opportunities that come with these sites' use of social media for journalism, and compare similarities and differences of traditional and digital-native journalists' social media uses. Based on data collected via a survey, interviews, focus groups, and a content analysis of Instagram posts, this chapter shows how independent, digital-native sites in Latin America employ social media in innovative ways that follow heterodox-creative logics (Mowbray, 2015), disrupting legacy journalism's normalized approach to social media, and thus orienting the sites toward the alternative.

Chapter 4 considers the role of gender and women journalists' contributions to the development of digital-native media as they contest the hegemony and sexism of traditional, "macho" media. Through interviews with the founders and journalists of independent, *cause-based* digital-native sites in Latin America doing journalism with a feminist or gender-focused lens, this chapter shows how a feminist gaze influences everything from why these sites were launched, to their news content and reporting practices, to their hiring practices and newsroom culture, including their approaches to mental health and physical safety. This feminist gaze orients these sites toward activism as well as professional journalism, yet clearly demarcates them from traditional, mainstream media.

Rooted in scholarly research on alternative and popular media in Latin America, Chapter 5 uses focus groups and interviews with journalists at independent, online-native sites, as well as a textual analysis of the sites' webpages, to explore what "alternative" means in Latin America's digital-native mediasphere. This chapter shows how these sites' critiques of traditional mainstream media, their commitment to covering and including marginalized communities, their justice-driven approach to stories for social change and in the public's interest, and their self-perceptions about identity represent a new journalistic model that moves beyond being alternative or mainstream.

Chapter 6 considers who is reading these independent, digital-native sites, and why. Based on a survey of readers, this chapter offers demographic information, news reading habits, political behaviors, and motivations of these sites' audiences. Ultimately this chapter contends that these digital-native news organizations' understanding of what they do is reflected not only by how their readers perceive them but also by how readers' use of these sites is tied to online and offline political participation.

In Chapter 7, the final chapter, I return to the main aim of the book, which is to show how independent, digital-native news sites in Latin America are fulfilling a role distinct from that of traditional, mainstream news media, and going beyond that of traditional alternative media in the region. The conclusion offers criteria as a heuristic to better understand the tensions between these sites' discursive orientations toward professional journalism/mainstream media and performance orientations toward activism/alternative media. Ultimately, this last chapter ends with a discussion of what the role of journalism should be in social change and whether digital-native sites in Latin America are fulfilling that responsibility.

A note on ethnocentrism

Although positivists assume there is a single, objective "truth," no research can be completely objective or bias-free, so the aim of research then becomes to learn about "contingent truths," which presuppose that a researcher's own experiences and perspectives impact the research (Rubin & Rubin, 2005). As researchers, we must take care that our own subjectivities inform, but do not distort, our interpretations. One such distortion particularly relevant to this book is ethnocentrism, as I am not from Latin America.

Ethnocentrism is the demonstration of "a lack of acceptance of cultural diversity, a general intolerance for outgroups and relative preference for one's ingroup over most outgroups" (Berry & Kalin, 1995, p. 303). Descriptions of what researchers observe while in the field must "appreciate local meanings and concerns," avoiding the temptation to place familiar—yet inapplicable—categories, criteria, standards, or meanings on the subjects under study (Emerson et al., 1995, p. 109).

Part of avoiding ethnocentrism herein requires relying on the decades of scholarship produced by Latin American scholars about alternative media. Flores-Márquez (2021) noted the importance of decolonization in popular communication research: "Latin American scholars resisted the Anglo and Eurocentric theoretical production, by exploring, analyzing and explaining their own context, by reformulating or discussing concepts, and particularly by articulating the practical projects with the theoretical production" (p. 192). However, despite the strength of the field for Latin America, it was marginalized in communication and media scholarship, which was dominated by the Global North (Suzina, 2021). Internationalizing media research means not just de-Westernizing existing concepts, but "generating an entirely new discourse whose reference points are, from the outset, global" (Couldry, 2007, p. 249). As such, I have made a concerted effort to situate my research within the long trajectory of communications research from Latin America.

Also crucial to avoiding ethnocentrism is "reflexivity," or the recognition that a researcher's "account does not mirror reality, but rather creates or constitutes as real whatever it describes" (Emerson et al., 1995, p. 213). Reflexivity requires being critically self-aware, understanding that "the ethnographic productions of such a self and the 'cultural other' are always historically and culturally contingent" (Foley, 2002, p. 473). Reflexivity can be confessional (where the researcher's personal experiences are central to the story), theoretical (where theory is grounded in the everyday practices and culture of the specific subjects under study), epistemological/intertextual (about critically analyzing the discipline, the theoretical developments within that discipline, and the discipline's influence on researchers' interpretations), or deconstructive (involving tearing down the supposedly objective constructs of the "cultural other" to critique notions of power, hierarchies, and privilege) (Foley, 2002; Marcus, 1994). The latter three have all been essential for this book.

As part of my own process of reflexivity, my decade spent as a reporter in the United States and Latin America, and my educational background in journalism, Spanish, Portuguese, and Latin American studies become particularly relevant for the ways in which they influenced my research on digital-native news sites throughout Latin America. The questions I posed, and the ways journalists responded, are contingent on our different—and shared—experiences and backgrounds. My experiences—as a freelancer in Guatemala, as a student researching journalism and clientelism in Brazil, as an Inter-American Foundation Grassroots development fellow studying alternative media in El Salvador, or as the blog editor for the Knight Center for Journalism in the Americas—and the personal and professional relationships I made along the way with journalists and activists throughout the region, all have bearing on this book and the research that went into it.

Notes

1 Salaverría and Corzo (2020) contended that *El Faro* was not the first digital-native site in the region. They cited an online newsletter from Nicaragua, Notifax, founded in 1995, as well as the now extinct *Ciberdiario de Nicaragua*, founded in 1996.
2 www.nuevosmedios.es
3 Throughout this book, the use of journalists' names varies depending on Institutional Review Board protocols that were approved at the time of the research. Founders/directors/editors who were interviewed are referred to by their real full names, and on subsequent reference by their last names. First-name only pseudonyms are used for all other journalists interviewed. Additionally, all focus group participants, whether founders or not, are referred to by pseudonyms, and the names of their sites were omitted, per IRB approval.
4 Between 2011 and 2021, I conducted 97 in-depth, semi-structured interviews in person or via Zoom with mainstream, digital-native, and alternative journalists and activists located in Argentina, Ecuador, El Salvador, Guatemala, Honduras, Mexico, and Venezuela. In 2011, I spent three months observing the daily operations of *El Faro* in El Salvador, and returned for brief stints in 2014 and 2017.

2 Online Journalism's "Super Pioneers": Entrepreneurship, Innovation, and the Case of Mexico

When Francisco Alanís founded Mexico's digital-native news site *Sopitas* in 2005, his goal, according to the site's webpage, was to "offer an alternative and independent information and entertainment channel to a generation that has been forgotten by traditional media." At first, he told me during an interview, he had been hesitant to consider himself an entrepreneur, an identity he had trouble reconciling with independent journalism. He associated entrepreneurialism with wanting to make money, and he aimed to "create his dream media outlet," not become a millionaire. Plus, he said, being an entrepreneur meant looking for investors, and "the biggest fear with investment funds is you don't know who is behind the money at the end of the day."

Alanís is not alone in his uncertainty about whether he qualified as an "entrepreneur"—after all, he started *Sopitas* without a business plan, and knew nothing about running a business, he said. In fact, most of Latin America's independent, digital-native news sites started without a business plan (Meléndez Yúdico, 2016) and are playing catch-up to their mainstream counterparts in terms of their business acumen (Salaverría, 2016). For example, Lizbeth Hernández, who helped start Mexico's *Kaja Negra* in 2010, said she had no business training, and everything about running a digital-native news site—from the digital tools themselves to the administrative side of things—she had to learn iteratively along the way, through experimentation, failure, and talking to others who were also figuring things out as they went. All she knew, she told me, was the kind of journalism she wanted to do: "From the beginning we wanted to be a media outlet that was active in the community we belong to … I was concerned about what I read in (Mexican) media and didn't like what I saw." The media ignored most of the country's population, and failed to explain the lived experiences that come with such a violent country, she said. Mexico has so many independent, digital-native news startups,

DOI: 10.4324/9781003152477-2

Hernández said, because others like her saw an opening—a *need*—for a different kind of journalism to serve different sectors of the community. Because of this community focus, she said, she considered herself more of a "self-starter" than an entrepreneur. Likewise, *Pie de Página* founder Daniela Pastrana said creating her site was a "pragmatic" decision in order to cover violence and do the kind of journalism most Mexican media shied away from. "I'm an entrepreneur because it allows me to continue being a journalist," she said.

Digital entrepreneurial journalism in Mexico opens up spaces to discuss violence in ways that aren't afforded in traditional, market-oriented media, with their history of clientelism and journalists as targets. For example, González de Bustamante and Relly's (2021) extensive research about U.S.-Mexico border journalism found violence created a disconnect between journalists' principles and practices, such as wanting to serve the public interest but limiting their reporting in the face of threats.

In in-depth interviews I conducted in 2017 with 16 journalists working at 12 digital-native news startups in Mexico City, participants in part attributed the existence of independent, entrepreneurial sites to violence against journalists, thus advancing González de Bustamante and Relly's (2021) work examining the ways in which violence impacts journalism practices and professional identities. In my interviews, participants recognized that the constraints of reporting placed on mainstream journalists by organized crime, drug trafficking, and government corruption necessitated an alternative approach. As Pastrana wrote on her *Pie de Página* bio page, she founded the news site looking "to change the narrative of terror installed in the Mexican press."

Violence thus provided journalists with an entrepreneurial opportunity: the normative reason for being that these digital-native sites needed. Covering violence, drug trafficking, and corruption—issues that other media typically can't or won't cover, journalists said—was a way to demonstrate their independence and commitment to society and to a "better" type of journalism, thus disarticulating them from mainstream journalism. For example, Mael Vallejo, then-general editor of *Animal Político,* said he left a major mainstream newspaper for the digital-native site because "here a different kind of journalism can be done ... The decision to come to *Animal Político* was to be able to do independent journalism in a country where it's very complicated to do independent journalism." He went on to explain:

> We believe that journalism has a social reason for being, that it supports and generates democracy. Creating this information,

discovering corruption, showing the violence that this country lives—and not just showing it but also explaining it—we understand that information is necessary for democracy and for making positive social change.

Entrepreneurial opportunity

Approaching violence as an entrepreneurial opportunity is emblematic of the innovation of Latin America's digital-native news sites. This chapter uses interviews, focus groups, and surveys to explore how these sites' innovations in financial and editorial independence are building a new agenda, challenging traditional media, and pioneering a new, entrepreneurial journalistic identity distinguishing them from mainstream media.

Entrepreneurship has been defined as the "discovery, evaluation, and exploitation of profitable opportunities" (Shane & Venkataraman, 2000, p. 218). Opportunities arise when inefficiencies or deficiencies are detected, when something new is created, or when existing resources are repurposed (Drucker, 1985). When innovation is brought into the mix, opportunities become entrepreneurial.

Rogers (1995), in his seminal work on the diffusion of innovations, defined innovation as "an idea, practice, or object that is perceived as new" (p. 11). Unlike inventions, which involve combining existing ideas and objects into something new, innovation revolves around taking something that exists and applying it to a new context (Storsul & Krumsvik, 2013). Products, processes, and even paradigms all can be innovated. Pavlik (2013) highlighted four dimensions of innovation within journalism, all of which can be found in Latin America's digital-native sites:

> (1) creating, delivering and presenting quality news content, (2) engaging the public in an interactive news discourse, (3) employing new methods of reporting optimized for the digital, networked age, and (4) developing new management and organizational strategies for a digital, networked and mobile environment. (p. 183)

Importantly, not all innovations have to completely topple our ways of thinking and acting. Innovations can be incremental or sustaining, or radical and disruptive (Christensen, 2003; Schumpeter, 1943). In fact, within entrepreneurial journalism scholarship, research shows most innovations are limited and gradual. Open Society Foundation's (OSF) global research into 35 media startups, including some in

Mexico and Brazil, concluded there was no "single groundbreaking innovation that is turning the world upside down" (Robinson et al., 2015, p. 11). It's also important to remember that as new or different as an innovation may be, its value ultimately is tied to its potential economic benefits and its promise of sustainability.

That holy grail of sustainable business models for digital media, though, has yet to be found. Around the world, entrepreneurial news organizations are juggling multiple revenue streams, testing out innovative financing means, and relying less and less on traditional advertising models and increasingly turning to a non-profit-oriented model dependent on philanthropic funding and donations. Foundation funding, though, cannot be sustained long term (Powers & Yaros, 2012). And while foundation funding of non-profit outlets around the globe does not necessarily directly interfere with content, it does still have an impact on journalists' roles (such as requiring them to take on administrative or marketing duties), practices (doing more with less), and even content (focusing on specific themes or topics to meet the requirements of grants) (Scott et al., 2019).

Whether they are officially non-profit, or for-profit outlets that put most revenues back into the journalism they produce, news startups in Latin America are particularly dependent on a foundation model or just a few funding sources, all of which can adversely affect their potential for sustainability, as well as their independence (Requejo-Alemán & Lugo-Ocando 2014). These sites share important similarities across countries: they claim economic and editorial independence from any commercial or political elite pressure, and they stake their identities on a distinct brand of journalism different from traditional, corporate media. Many are investigative in nature, or are cause-based, championing feminism, human rights, or democracy.

Sustainability and innovation

The first half of the 2010 decade in particular saw an explosion in the number of new digital-native news sites. Most journalists I interviewed attributed this growth to the failings of mainstream media—they started their sites, as both Alanís and Hernández noted at the start of this chapter, to establish new and different ways of doing journalism that would counteract what traditional media did, and make up for what they didn't do. This is in line with the OSF report (Robinson et al., 2015), which found news startups around the globe were mostly launched to fill a societal need. Importantly, though, most of these sites—globally and in Latin America—were started by journalists, not business people, and were launched online because the cost of creating a print outlet was prohibitive. Like news startups around the world, the Latin American sites continue to grapple with sustainability. Part of what might be considered a financial disadvantage compared with mainstream media comes from the fact that most digital-native sites shun political, and sometimes commercial, advertising, and rely instead on multiple revenue streams, like foundation funding, merchandising, reader donations, and membership fees (Harlow, 2021a; Tejedor et al., 2020). However, scalability is tied to advertising, thus limiting the reach of many of these outlets.

These challenges related to sustainability are not all negative, though: they have spurred innovative ways of thinking about journalism and business models, helping these online, entrepreneurial sites cultivate their identities as different than traditional media. In focus groups[1] I helped conduct, journalists perceived themselves as "super pioneers," clearing the path for a different, more innovative, and better kind of journalism in the region. "The innovation is in various aspects of journalism, and I think we're super pioneers," as Carla, from Brazil, said. Journalists saw themselves as pioneers in multiple new frontiers—technology, financial models, content and counternarratives, audience relationships, and even journalistic norms. The very way they defined "innovation" spoke to their identities as pioneers forging a new understanding of quality journalism, disarticulating them from the practices and values of traditional, corporate, mainstream news media. Journalists' use of "pioneering" to describe their roles and practices in 2015 illustrates how pioneering they actually are: six years later, Hepp and Loosen (2021), based on interviews with European and U.S. journalists, referred to the concept of "pioneer journalists" who, whether in established media outlets, news startups, or as individuals, are "dedicated to stimulating innovative journalistic forms" to "build an imagined future for journalism" (p. 582). Latin America's independent, digital-native news pioneers indeed are such forerunners for a different kind of journalism, experimenting with different business models and approaches to storytelling, and innovating new ways of thinking about normative roles and responsibilities, as they forge a path toward sustainability.

Technology

When talking about innovation during focus groups, Latin American journalists repeatedly used the phrase "beyond technology." They experimented with new technologies and digital tools, and were always looking for new ways to use social media. But quintessentially, they suggested innovation meant going beyond which technologies are used, and being creative in terms of funding and content in order to maintain financial and editorial independence—something journalists agreed was lacking in mainstream media. "I would say it's not so much the technological innovation that distinguishes us, but our strength is the independence of our voice," Oscar from Nicaragua said. At its core, innovation means not doing something just for the sake of newness, but "aspiring to quality journalism, looking for greater impact on the community," Luís from El Salvador said. It's important to note, though, that these journalists' insistence that innovation entailed so much more than just technology could be related to one of the main weaknesses of digital-native media: they lack legacy media's "technological resources, the most extensive and experienced teams, the largest economic funds, and the most well-known brands" (Salaverría & Corzo, 2020, p. 158).

Despite this, journalists in the focus groups were confident in their innovativeness, something backed up by results from an online survey[2] of Latin American journalists I helped conduct. Results showed significantly more journalists from digital-native media than from traditional, mainstream media said they and their outlets were innovative (Table 2.1). Innovation thus was intrinsic to their creation of a distinct identity separating them from other journalists and outlets.

Table 2.1 Differences in perceptions of innovation, by type of outlet where journalists work

Innovativeness	Traditional, mainstream media M (SD)	Digital-native media M (SD)	Significant difference t (d.f.)
Own outlet innovative	2.90 (1.19)	**3.47 (1.19)**	−7.18 (895.04)***
Outlet more innovative than others	2.84 (1.29)	**3.13 (1.27)**	−3.484 (897.85)***
Self-perception as more innovative than other journalists	3.58 (.97)	**3.75 (1.05)**	−2.55 (895.94)*

Note: Values are means with standard deviations in parentheses. Perceptions of innovativeness were measured on a scale of 1 (low) to 5 (high). Bold font indicates statistically significant differences for that media type.

* $p < .05$,
*** $p < .001$.

Journalists' views on innovation are important, especially since alternative media historically have been viewed as more innovative and creative than mainstream media (Downing, 2001). These sites' efforts toward innovating can be construed as a disarticulation from the mainstream. It is important, though, to consider how journalists define innovation, given that they see it as a fundamental boundary separating them from traditional media. Analysis of the focus group discussions in combination with survey results revealed three main ways journalists defined innovation as characteristic of their distinct, digital-native identities: (1) financial independence, (2) editorial independence, and the embracing of (3) participatory and collaborative news values.

Funding

These Latin American journalists said their *financial independence* is part of what made them innovative. The history of media clientelism in countries like Argentina, Brazil, Mexico, and Peru, as well as the continued governmental harassment of journalists in El Salvador, Nicaragua, and Venezuela, help explain journalists' wariness of any kind of financing that might curtail their independence. As Luís from El Salvador said during the focus group discussions, independence depends on economic sustainability, making innovation in financing all the more important. Journalists noted that they depended on multiple revenue streams—like crowdfunding, events, and merchandise—but that commercial advertising was limited, and government advertising was avoided. If you have to rely on government funding, then the government will dictate your editorial agenda, said Ricardo from Mexico. Government funding interferes with independence, Marina from Brazil said, but the flipside is that being independent interferes with sustainability, limiting their funding options.

When discussing financial independence, journalists talked about being "freed" from business and political ties or having the "weight" of commercial interests lifted from them. "We're trying to go for an economic model outside commercial media, because what they're doing today is an old solution for a new problem," Carla said. "We're looking for new forms of sustainability, and that's innovative, reinventing the economic model for journalistic production." Sergio from Peru said that the freedom from commercial interests "has founded a new type of journalism." In other words, liberation from the profit-driven focus of legacy media opened innovative possibilities for new types of funding models that would allow for a different model of journalism free from elite manipulation. Journalists in the focus groups noted that, unlike their mainstream counterparts, they didn't have to worry about commercial and political interests getting in the way of covering what needed to be reported. They could "go beyond the limits of traditional media," Catalina from Venezuela said, highlighting the novelty of these sites' ability to investigate in-depth the sectors that typically sustain commercial media.

Survey results also showed digital-native journalists valued financial independence. Somewhat surprising, though, was the lack of significant difference between type of outlet journalists worked for, and their belief in the importance of financial independence. On a scale of 1–5, where 1 meant not important at all and 5 meant extremely important, journalists across the board reported a mean importance of 4.49. Even journalists working at traditional outlets recognized the need for financial independence, regardless of whether their outlets actually were free from financial ties to political and business elites. The innovation, then, lies in the practice, and not merely the appreciation, of financial independence.

Economic independence, when viewed as a form of innovation, fits well within traditional conceptions of alternative media. Alternative journalism's "critiques of the political economy and ideological practices of professional journalism" (Atton & Hamilton, 2008, p. 138) indicate a disavowal of commercial support and the pressures that come with it. Still, many alternative projects have experimented with commercial advertising. Forde's (2011) research in the United States, U.K., and Australia showed that more than whether an outlet is commercial, what matters are the motives behind commercial success: alternative journalism isn't seeking large profits to assuage shareholders or enrich owners like in mainstream media, but rather any money made is used to pay the bills and invest in better journalism. Journalists from the digital-native sites made clear that quality journalism, not profit, was their priority—profit was just the necessary condition enabling them to do the different, innovative journalism they were so proud of. As El Salvador's *El Faro's* website says, it's not that the site, which only gets about 18% of its budget from advertisements or sponsorships, is inherently opposed to commercial financing, but rather that the "market for independent journalism" has not really developed. In other words, businesses don't see a financial benefit in advertising in an independent news outlet that doesn't play by the mainstream rules favoring elites and the status quo. *El Faro's* observation is an important one, as it suggests an underlying incompatibility between the interests of advertisers and those of independent journalism.

Content

Financial independence gives these sites *editorial independence*, journalists said. While in interviews several journalists from various Latin American countries acknowledged that foundation funding and international foundations' interests in promoting justice and human rights indirectly influenced digital-native startups' content focus (in line with what Scott et al.'s 2019 study showed), they were adamant it played no part in how stories were covered. The sites' editorial independence is innovative, journalists said during focus groups, because their editorial lines and agendas look nothing like those of mainstream media. Journalists perceived traditional, corporate media as continuing to publish the same old types of stories with the same sources as always—stories that support the interests of political and financial elites and further the status quo. In contrast, they saw digital-native sites as innovating via disruption, decentering elite perspectives from the traditional media agenda as they set their own new agenda. Amanda from Chile said the sites' different approach to content is "capable of changing the standards, capable of generating changes in the agenda. By showing that which the rest of media organizations are not showing, you can be successful." Similarly, Sergio said they cover what other media "don't dare to cover," whether drug traffickers, corrupt politicians, or the commercial sector. Part of innovating content requires quoting different sources, Marina said. They bring in Indigenous voices, and view the public as a partner, she said, which results in a new kind of content, able to reach new audiences. Ricardo said that the differences between the digital-native sites and mainstream media need to be thought of as independent vs. official/propagandistic media, as what traditional media were producing wasn't actually news. Such comments suggested these journalists saw their content as *real* journalism, while that of traditional media was something else altogether.

Despite some editorial overlap between mainstream and alternative journalism, research points to key content differences between the two genres, such as when it comes to mainstream media's overreliance on authorities as sources, or alternative media's prioritization of grassroots storytelling approaches (Atton & Wickenden, 2005; Harcup, 2013). Alternative content, unlike mainstream, tends to be more radical, critical of the status quo, and more often and more favorably covers civil society, activist issues, protests, and social movements (Downing, 2001; Holt et al., 2019; McLeod & Hertog, 1999). Some research also points to more content similarities between news stories produced by alternative media and by digital-native outlets, than between digital-native and mainstream stories (Kilgo et al., 2018).

For example, a content analysis I conducted of 600 protest-related news stories in Guatemala and El Salvador showed articles in traditional, mainstream media quoted significantly more officials as sources (36%) than did stories in digital-native media (22%), which quoted significantly more protesters (36%) than did their mainstream counterparts (30%). Traditional, mainstream stories also used more negative depictions of protesters, and focused more on confrontations between police and protesters (33%), than stories in digital-native outlets (17%). These findings offer valuable evidence to support journalists' discourse about producing news content that differs from that found in traditional media.

Survey results showed journalists from the digital-native outlets were significantly more likely than those from traditional outlets to say they had freedom to choose what they covered (Figure 2.1). If journalists at digital-native sites don't feel constrained by what they're permitted to cover, it's no wonder, then, that their discourse points to news narratives and practices that defy traditional, mainstream models. It follows that

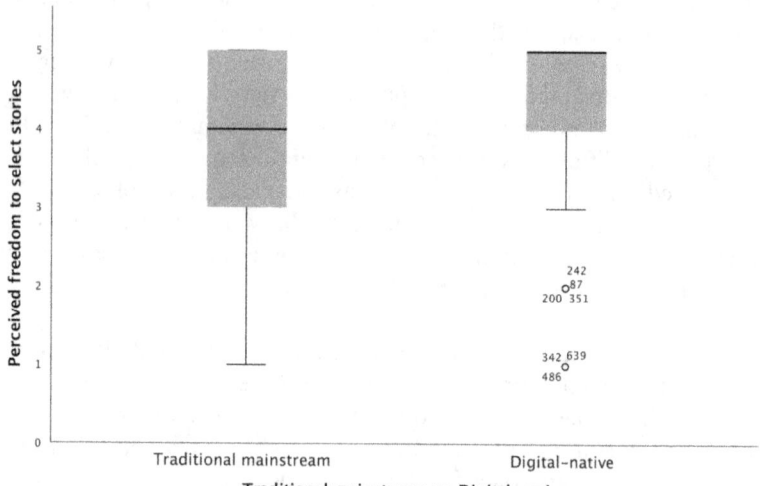

Figure 2.1 Comparison of perceptions about freedom to choose stories among journalists at traditional and digital-native outlets.

Note: Means are calculated using a 1–5 scale, where 5 = completely free. Average mean for journalists at traditional outlets was 3.80, SD = 1.12; and for journalists at digital-native sites, the mean was 4.26, SD = 1.04. $t(546.76) = -4.83$, $p < .001$.

editorial freedom might encourage journalists to further innovate in terms of including new and counter- topics, voices, and narratives. This innovative perception of editorial freedom among digital-native sites bolsters the contention that these sites are disarticulated from the mainstream. Interestingly, survey results did not show significant differences between how journalists from traditional media and digital-native media viewed the importance of innovating in content (topics covered), editorial independence, or the variety of sources/voices quoted. Just like with the value they placed on financial independence, journalists generally ascribed importance to editorial independence, despite the clientelist ties between news companies and political and economic elites. This points to the digital-native sites as practicing the values journalists generally want, suggesting these sites could potentially serve as a blue-print for traditional, corporate outlets if mainstream journalists start demanding the financial and editorial independence they say they value. In other words, journalists—whether or not they work for digital-native sites—seemingly are articulated toward alternative journalism's values of editorial independence and plurality of voices. Perhaps, then, it's not necessarily that these are alternative values, so much as ideal journalistic ones that have gotten lost in Latin America's overly clientelist, concentrated, commercially driven media system. As Pastrana said, rather than constantly coming up with new labels to describe journalism that's different than the mainstream, it's time to reclaim the values and practices that comprise what *real* journalism *should* be, as the independent digital-native sites are doing.

Participation, collaboration

Innovation also lies in *using emerging technologies to create relationships* that go beyond what traditional media offer, journalists said. They don't just give readers a chance to like and share content on social media, but they're actively working to incorporate readers' ideas, opinions, and voices into the journalism process in new ways that hearken back to the goals of community and alternative media. Including audiences and making them feel like part of a community is also likely linked to the fact that many of these organizations rely on reader paid memberships, and creating a sense of belonging is key to maintaining audience funding as a revenue stream (Harlow, 2021a). Unlike commercial media, journalists said, they value audiences for more than the social metrics and web traffic they offer. Journalists saw themselves as offering a public service that audiences could use to better inform themselves, and improve their communities. They viewed readers not only as co-creators in the journalistic process but also as fellow members of their community.

Lidia from Argentina commented, "We're innovative because of public involvement; it's a community effort. In our case, the characteristic that makes us innovative is that we think of the entire information production process as collective." Eduardo from Venezuela explained that his outlet is innovative because journalists see news as a "permanent, live, ongoing conversation with the public." Such public involvement would never be possible—technologically or otherwise—at a traditional journalism outlet, he said. Additionally, Claudia from Brazil said, "The commitment of our readers is an index of success for us." Getting as many people involved as possible could lead to "what could be a different journalism," Catalina speculated.

Journalists' views about the value of participation align with the "participatory ethos of alternative media" (Harcup, 2013, p. 135). This participation, enabled by technology, goes beyond letters to the editor or social media comments on a news story to focus on interaction and engagement, encouraging audiences not just to read or share a story, but to use that information to empower themselves and participate in a larger public debate that the news sites are leading, as Luís said.

Beyond bolstering audience involvement, these sites are also pioneering relationships with community organizations, advocacy groups, social movements, and even other—alternative—media outlets, making collaboration another constitutive characteristic of what makes them innovative in ways that are different from traditional media. Collaboration, like audience participation, opens these sites up to claims of bias since bringing new voices into the journalism process doesn't necessarily pay homage to traditional conceptions of objectivity. For these journalists, collaborating with social movements and alternative media often meant taking a stand against injustice, and aligning with certain causes, like human rights, LGBTQ+ rights, and the right to freedom of expression. As Catalina said, "we want to do a journalism we believe in." Elena from Peru explained:

> We've created a network of journalists that are against homophobia and want to provide LGBTQ information in Latin America … Our innovation, beyond technology, is based in collaborative work and we've managed to forge alliances with civil society to do this kind of journalism that is not very common in Peru and Latin America in general.

Against the current

Journalists' discussions about being innovative and different from traditional media were premised on the recognition that their innovations in financial and editorial independence were made possible by digital technology and the ability to seek everything from online public opinion to online public donations. Sergio said,

> All of us here have come from the traditional press and we have found that [in the traditional press] there were very serious obstacles to be able to carry out journalistic expression in the way our society needs. So ... the internet and new technologies have been fundamental for quality content.

Amanda noted that getting audiences to read serious content online means using the same tools that produce "cat photos, memes, things that are very commercial, salable," so it's a delicate balance, and requires "going against the current."

These sites go against the current—whether that of traditional, corporate news media or the commercialized internet culture—in order to set a different agenda. Even as journalism in the region professionalizes and journalists' role perceptions shift—at least in rhetoric if not practice—more toward the neutral, disseminator role (Mellado et al., 2017), for these digital-native sites, the interventionist role—to intentionally set the agenda (Higgins Joyce, 2018)—is fundamental to their identities as innovative and independent. Unlike conventional conceptions of interventionist or advocacy roles, these journalists don't want to set an agenda that is partisan or favors a particular political party or social movement. As survey results showed, journalists from digital-native sites still valued traditional norms like neutrality, or the belief that journalists shouldn't participate in activism. At the same time, though, they saw their role as using their digital-ness to challenge traditional ways of doing journalism that, journalists said, are not only outdated, but ignore the public interest. Their interventionism, then, centers citizens and democracy. As Paola from El Salvador explained, "It's a different type of journalism, not just because it's online, but because of what we prioritize and how we report, freely. We're pioneers in this area, not just because we're digital ... Being digital just gives journalists the freedom to do the kind of journalism we want." Journalists thus saw their "super" pioneering, innovative approaches to funding, content, and collaboration as creating new ways to think about journalism and its role in society.

Digital-native journalists' commitment to innovation in terms of financial and editorial independence, stories that cover the topics and voices excluded by mainstream media, and participation and collaboration are hallmarks more of ideal-types of alternative rather than mainstream media (Harlow, 2021b). Journalists' discussions about their roles and setting a new agenda point to important deviations from traditional journalistic norms and practices, disarticulating them from traditional, mainstream journalism. These Latin American journalists easily fit into the journalistic entrepreneurial identity of *Guardian* (Harlow & Chadha, 2019) because of the way their innovativeness—in sustainability, independence, and going against the current to set a new agenda—is aimed at remaking journalism—challenging traditional ways of doing and funding journalism in order to achieve an enhanced, more professional journalism. These sites, then, are at the margins not just of mainstream media, but also alternative media—an innovation in and of itself.

Mexico: Violence as an entrepreneurial opportunity

Mexico provides a rich case for better understanding how digital-native sites' innovation in financing, content, and participation positions them as professional journalism oriented toward alternative media, challenging mainstream media from the margins. When writing this chapter in 2021, SembraMedia[3] had identified more than 800 independent, entrepreneurial, digital-native news organizations throughout Latin America, 124 of which were in Mexico, the country with the largest share of such sites. Mexico continues to be one of the world's most dangerous countries for journalists because of organized crime, government corruption, and a weak judicial system. Its concentrated media system and a broadcast licensing system unfavorable toward community media result in a lack of media pluralism. Reporters Without Borders, in its global press freedom rankings of 180 countries, placed Mexico in 143rd place—about par with Pakistan (145th) and Russia (150th), and among Latin American countries, only Venezuela, Honduras, and Cuba were ranked lower. Independent, online journalism thus comes with risks—not just in entrepreneurial, financial terms and the uncertainties associated with ever-evolving technologies, but also personal risks because of the rampant violence against journalists and impunity in Mexico.

How journalists at digital-native sites in Mexico frame risks and discuss violence[4] sheds light on their differential articulations toward or away from mainstream media. As noted at the start of this chapter, violence can be viewed as an entrepreneurial opportunity to produce a different kind of journalism. For example, Hernández from *Kaja Negra* said journalists had a "responsibility" to understand and cover violence. *Kaja Negra* was created to fill that gap in coverage left by commercial media's inability, or unwillingness, to cover Mexico's reality, she said. Similarly, another site, *Pie de Página*, was designed to be a "refuge for journalists who couldn't publish in other places," Pastrana said. She said the site has "a position that's very political, very clear, which is a journalism to strengthen democracy, human rights, and cover the people's agenda." It's difficult to do journalism this way, she said, because it means prioritizing the voice of the people over politicians, whereas most media in Mexico do the opposite. Juan Pablo de Leo also said that his venture, *Político Mx*, was created because he loves journalism and loves politics, but that covering the "reality" of Mexico meant it was "hard to do journalism without compromising yourself on a lot of occasions" and he wanted to have the "freedom" to do what he loved without being subject to any of the outside influences that might dictate what journalism looks like. "It sounds like I'm very idealistic, no?" he said, adding that in Mexico, it's "an act of rebellion" to do independent journalism. Ernesto Ledesma, director of *Rompeviento TV,* said he decided to "run the (financial and personal) risk" of launching an independent site because he realized that mainstream, commercial media "were not going to generate the social conscience that would wake up—that would help—people to react in the face of so much crime, so much corruption, so much impunity."

When it came to financial independence and how journalism should be funded, Mexican journalists' perspectives were filtered through a violence lens. Investigating violence and corruption automatically means losing out on revenues from commercial businesses and the state, journalists said. As such, they have to find alternative ways of funding independent journalism without commercial or government advertising. For example, de Leo said the digital site he helped found rejects government advertising, because otherwise "how would we be able to have any influence or credibility?" Unlike mainstream media, *Animal Político* is not dependent on advertising and doesn't have an editorial line that's tied to the government or a particular political party, which means journalists can cover violence and corruption with the goal of diminishing it and holding power accountable, Vallejo said. Without advertising, journalists said, their sites have published paid content from community organizations, created events—workshops, parties, and even festivals—and partnered with restaurants and other businesses as a way to bring in revenues. A few have tried crowdfunding and reader donation campaigns. All acknowledged the need for multiple revenue streams in order to be sustainable, and because of the violence, part of sustainability means paying journalists at these sites more than they would get working for traditional, mainstream media. Pastrana explained that in Mexico it's common for journalists to take on side jobs—often working for the government—which not only creates conflicts of interest but also puts journalists at risk and limits what they can cover, especially when it comes to trying to disentangle violence. To free them of such a "trap," she said, her digital site pays them more.

Violence also drives content at digital-native sites, but differently than at mainstream outlets, where coverage is constrained by political and economic ties, as well as threats and pressure from organized crime. For the independent, digital-native sites, rather than limited by violence, they are empowered to find ways to meaningfully respond to it. Covering violence meant de-centering the voices and perspectives that mainstream media typically focus on, journalists said, by focusing on their public interest mission and bringing forward the viewpoints of the most "invisible of the invisible," as Pastrana phrased it. Journalists also talked about the creation of collaborations across digital outlets in response to the violence, enabling expensive and complicated investigations and broadening individual outlets' reach and impact. While only a few of the interviewed journalists mentioned actively protesting violence, they saw the networks they created as a way to use the tools of journalism to fight violence and corruption, such as through emergency alerts about and help for threatened or attacked journalists. As Hernández explained, stories about immigration, human trafficking, drug trafficking, and corruption are not unique to Mexico, so collaborating across countries, as well as with local media outlets within Mexico's interior, helps provide better coverage and a deeper understanding of the reality of violence. Importantly, doing so also lends to the development of a collective narrative, or collective memory. She said,

> We have worked a lot on the issues of violence because we believe that to understand the human rights problem, we must understand what violence is in our country. If we do not understand that, then we will continue, instead of helping to explain it, we will continue to reproduce it.

Journalists also recognized that by being located in the capital, they were in somewhat of a protected "bubble." While they were not totally free from threats or attacks, they said, their location afforded them somewhat of an advantage to be able to report on violence in ways that journalists in smaller communities—often under the control of organized crime groups—could not.

Ultimately, Mexican journalists' responses to violence were bound up in their identity as independent journalists. They attributed much of their sites' success to their financial and editorial independence. Relatively low pay, corruption, and safety issues meant their professional identity as journalists with a social responsibility became all the more important. They take risks because journalism matters, they said, and if they don't do it, who will? After all, most of the journalists interviewed talked about the need for their sites to exist because of the sheer lack of coverage reflecting Mexico's reality. In fact, the centrality of violence to these digital-native sites is evidenced by many of their names: *Plumas Atómicas* (atomic pens), *Crash, Animal Político* (political animal). *Kaja Negra's* (black box) name is particularly telling: it references the black box on a plane that has crashed, recording the voices of those trying to make sense of what went wrong.

Conclusion

The interviews with journalists at digital-native sites in Mexico thus show how violence created an entrepreneurial opening for resistance to emerge in the form of financial and editorial innovation. Violence also severed many of these sites' financial and editorial connections—articulations—to mainstream media. Their paths toward sustainability and success are intertwined with their opposition to mainstream business and journalism models, as they valued financial independence alongside editorial content aimed not just at reporting on the violence, but denouncing and stopping it. Notably, their innovative independence is what made them more professional, in their view, than mainstream media journalists, who were hamstrung by the commercial and editorial limitations that come with practicing journalism in one of the region's most deadly countries. These sites' agency in choosing to cover violence, be critical of the systems enabling it, and push for change thus became an integral part of their distinctive identities, providing an example of how these sites are pioneering new ways of thinking about journalism and its societal role. Mexican digital-native news sites, by articulating toward professionalism within a dangerous context, while also orienting themselves toward non-mainstream values that prioritize the public's interest, thus re-orient our understanding of what mainstream and alternative journalism look like in times of violence. The case of Mexico is useful for illustrating how the financial, editorial, and participatory innovativeness of digital-native news sites across Latin America are changing the journalism landscape, offering a glimpse at a re-made model of what journalism in the region could ideally be: professional, financially and editorially independent, and yet with an alternative, social change- and justice-oriented agenda.

Notes

1 Three 60-minute online focus groups, two in Spanish and one in Portuguese, were conducted in 2015 by the research team of the Knight Center for Journalism in the Americas. Participants included 18 journalists (nine men and nine women) from leading independent, digital-native news sites in eight countries: Argentina, Brazil, Chile, El Salvador, Mexico, Nicaragua, Peru, and Venezuela.
2 The 2017 survey was sent to roughly 15,500 journalists, journalism educators, and journalism students who subscribed to the mailing list of the Knight Center for Journalism in the Americas. For the purposes of this book, the 1,094 journalist respondents from 20 countries were collapsed into two groups: mainstream media journalists who worked at broadcast TV, cable TV, commercial radio, newspapers, magazines, and news wires; and journalists who identified as working for digital-native outlets. Survey questions mentioned herein were measured on scales of 1 (low) to 5 (high).
3 https://directorio.sembramedia.org/el-ecosistema/
4 This analysis about violence in part is based on a conference presentation: Poepsel, M. & Harlow, S. (2017, October). *Digital journalism and entrepreneurship in Mexico* [conference presentation]. Global Fusion Consortium Conference, Athens, Ohio.

3 Social Media: Likes, Comments, Action!

Originally launched as a YouTube channel in 2014, Venezuela's *El Pitazo*—"whistleblowing"—was meant to, as its motto goes, "sound where others are silent" in a country with a dismal freedom of expression record. For *El Pitazo,* the most-blocked news site in Venezuela (Alvarado Mejias et al., 2019), social media offer a way to circumvent online censorship: if one platform goes down, there's always another one to get the news out.

For example, in 2020, when *El Pitazo's* YouTube channel was temporarily taken down, the site turned to its most popular social media platform, Instagram. "We invite all of our audience to take a position, make themselves heard with their voices so that the channel is fully restored," the site posted along with a video promising *El Pitazo* would return to "defend a journalism that is useful for forming opinion and to rebuilding democracy" and fulfill its "mission and responsibility to the audience."

In a country where independent journalism is seen as subversive and where the government has systematically shut down or co-opted most private media (López, 2021), independent news sites like *El Pitazo* recognize that not only do they have to disperse their content across social platforms, they also have to reach their audiences offline. So when YouTube or the main website gets blocked, to ensure the news gets out, *El Pitazo* mobilizes on social media, and offline "in the streets," hanging hand-written posters on the sides of buildings with the top news stories of the day, and sharing audio clips through loudspeakers from its network of "infocitizens," or community members trained to report on their neighborhoods.

El Pitazo's expansion from YouTube to Instagram, Facebook, WhatsApp, Telegram, and even analog posters, fliers, and loudspeakers is characteristic of the transmedia innovation and creativity of so many of the Latin American independent, digital-native news outlets

DOI: 10.4324/9781003152477-3

looking for new ways to tell stories and reach audiences across digital divides. In so doing, they're disrupting traditional media's normalization of social media (Lasorsa et al., 2012), pioneering norms and practices that distinguish their journalism from that of mainstream, corporate media. Falck and Barnes (1975) identified three types of behaviors that those seeking change can adopt: (1) normative behaviors, which offer new ideas that adapt to existing structures and change nothing; (2) deviant behaviors, which reject and try to replace the prevailing structures, but any potential changes are usually opposed for being too radical, again leading to little lasting change; and (3) non-normative behaviors, where, rather than accept or replace the existing structures, entirely new ideas are brought in, and thus are more likely to change the existing structures. These digital-native news sites' approach to social media can be viewed as non-normative behaviors—they're seeking change from within the structures of professional journalism, but outside the hegemonic constraints of traditional, mainstream media.

Take Ecuador's *BN Periodismo (BN Journalism)*: this digital-native news site came about after a group of friends who studied journalism at the same university couldn't find jobs in traditional media. They turned to social media to create their own jobs and own brand of journalism, launching *BN Periodismo* in 2017 on YouTube. As of 2021, *BN Periodismo* had developed into multiple platforms and even podcasts, but it remained entirely in the realm of social media. The outlet, while it goes by the more appropriate and PR-friendly name *BN Periodismo*, is named for the "beso negro" (black kiss), an intimate sexual act, because it offers "journalism that goes deep."

Such irreverence carries over into the site's journalism: they "follow the rules of journalism," but do so with humor. It's a "totally journalistic" format, as one of the founders explained in a podcast, but it's not for everyone, which is why it's on social media. "If you want to laugh, we'll inform you," he said. SembraMedia's directory of independent, digital-native sites[1] describes *BN Periodismo* as "born from the need to make fun of the political subjects that pull the strings in Ecuador … BN videos have an informative function with the dual intention of drawing laughter."

That dual function is fundamental to the "heterodox-creative logics of alternative media" (Mowbray, 2015). *BN Periodismo's* satirical and informational videos follow just such a logic, incorporating creativity, innovation, and aesthetics to reconfigure social media as a tool for critical disruption of hegemonic, mainstream media. Using a survey, interviews, focus groups, and a content analysis of Instagram posts, this chapter shows how independent, digital-native sites in Latin America use social media in ways that follow heterodox-creative logics, disrupting traditional journalism's approach to social media as they orient themselves toward the alternative.

Social media for journalism

Like elsewhere around the world, in Latin America social media have become central not just to journalistic practices but also political life (Mitchelstein et al., 2020). While social media contribute to the spread of misinformation and extremist hate speech, they also facilitate information diffusion as well as political and social participation; in fact, social media's negative effects have been "overblown" in research as scholars over-corrected to counterbalance exaggerated claims about the democratic potential of social media (Mitchelstein et al., 2020, p. 7). Constraints imposed by digital inequalities within and between countries—the average Internet penetration for Latin America and the Caribbean is 77%, ranging from a low of 37.6% in Honduras to a high of 92% in Chile (Internet World Stats, 2021)—have led to overly pessimistic assumptions about the value of online news and journalistic uses of social media. Yet, the high rates of mobile-phone penetration and mobile Internet use, and the creative ways news outlets connect offline audiences with online content—such as *El Pitazo* hanging up handwritten posters with the day's news—underline the need for non-digitally deterministic research that assumes neither automatic social benefits nor harm and that recognizes the limits and potential opportunities of institutionalizing social and digital journalism in the region.

Journalists' adoption of social media has not been uniform across Latin America. Uses vary by platform, country, and type of news outlet (Banegas Flores, 2016; García-Perdomo, 2021; Herscovitz, 2012; Saldaña et al., 2017; Yezers'ka & Zeta de Pozo, 2016). While research tends to view Latin America, its news media, and journalistic uses of social media as homogenous blocks, this chapter points to heterogeneity in social media uses not just between traditional and digital-native outlets but also across country and platform, helping us to better situate the mainstream and alternative articulations of these sites' social media practices.

Digital-native vs. mainstream

Understanding what is unique or innovative about digital-native sites' use of social media requires first considering how their use differs from traditional, corporate media's. Given that journalists at independent, digital-native sites tend to be oriented toward the mainstream in terms of professional training and practices, we should expect to see some commonalities in social media use among journalists from traditional media and digital-native outlets. We also might expect that, given the sites' emphasis on innovation (discussed in Chapter 2) and the fact that they are online-only, journalists from the digital-native sites might incorporate social media more than their legacy counterparts.

The 2017 survey of Latin American journalists I helped conduct sheds light on similarities and differences between how journalists from traditional and digital-native outlets use social media (Table 3.1). As expected, results showed greater Facebook and Twitter use among journalists working at digital-native sites than those working for traditional outlets like newspapers and television. However, working as a journalist at a digital-native site was related to lower frequency of WhatsApp use for journalism. The fact that WhatsApp was used more among traditional journalists could be related to the ubiquity of the app, which dominates messaging across Latin America. WhatsApp essentially has become institutionalized across social groups (Valenzuela et al., 2021), so perhaps it's no longer seen as an innovative tool for journalists, but rather just an everyday part of life.

The platform differences between journalists from digital-native and traditional outlets found in the survey are bolstered by interviews and focus groups, during which journalists from digital-native news sites emphasized the importance of using different social media strategies for different platforms to reach different audiences. Francisco Alanís from Mexico's *Sopitas* explained that whenever his site produces a story, journalists think about what kinds of content—whether a video, infographic, audio, or something else—can be added to best tell the story on each platform. It's not about transferring traditional formats to social media—normalization—but rather thinking about the affordances of each platform to innovate new story formats, journalists said. For example, Laura Aguirre from the Salvadoran site *Alharaca* said they use Instagram to create cards, or a series of explainer slides that provide in-depth information in the form of snackable bites that audiences expect from social media. These infographics drive traffic to the outlet's website, drawing readers to the full story, she said. The cards thus have become a new, Instagram-specific story format that uses marketing and social media principles to report the news in innovative ways.

Instagram was where journalists expressed the most excitement about the possibility of creativity. Most of their young, typically female, readers were on Instagram, as opposed to the older male readers

Table 3.1 Differences in frequency of social media use, by type of outlet where journalists work

Social media use	Traditional media	Digital-native media	Significant difference t (d.f.)
Frequency of Facebook use for work	4.18 (1.15)	**4.49 (.85)**	t = 2.549, df = 249.16
Frequency of Twitter use for work	4.15 (1.22)	**4.42 (1.09)**	t = −2.014, df = 273.49
Frequency of Instagram use for work	3.01 (1.51)	3.12 (1.56)	t = −.624, df = 283.27
Frequency of WhatsApp use for work	**4.72 (.77)**	4.32 (1.29)	t = 3.267, df = 245.63
Frequency of YouTube use for work	3.58 (1.15)	3.39 (1.27)	t = 1.31, df = 283.95
Use of social media for reporting	**2.87 (.76)**	2.7 (.73)	t = 2.02, df = 279.66
Use of social media for monitoring the news	1.81 (.30)	1.80 (.29)	t = .290, df = 280.70
Use of social media for branding	2.83 (.77)	**3.05 (.68)**	t = −2.473, df = 273.13

Note: Values are means with standard deviations in parentheses. Frequencies were measured on a scale of 1 (low) to 5 (high). Bold font indicates statistically significant differences between media types.

who frequented the websites—which meant they could stretch traditional journalistic boundaries on Instagram. "We write for different people on Instagram than on the webpage," said Milagro Mariona of the Argentine site *La Nota:*

> We know that the people consuming news stories on the webpage are there for stories that are longer, more complex, more in-depth. They're not the same people that click 'like' on a 15-second GIF on Instagram. I don't say this because one product is better than the other, but they're different. And that helps us to be innovators.

The visual storytelling affordances of Instagram allowed them to reach younger audiences who might not be as interested in traditional news, said Jennifer Ávila of the *ContraCorriente* site in Honduras. She explained that younger audiences have become accustomed to certain social media aesthetics, or etiquette, so they expect their news to correspond to what they're used to seeing on Instagram, which means journalists have to get creative in how they use emojis, filters, GIFs, and mashups to produce social media-worthy videos and stories.

Branding, reporting, monitoring

Building on previous research (Mourão & Harlow, 2020), survey results showed that Latin American journalists used social media for work in three main ways: *branding* (broadcasting live, publicizing their own work, communicating with readers, and receiving people's feedback; *reporting* (finding sources and ideas for news stories, conducting interviews, and receiving information from sources); and *monitoring the news* (to keep up with the news and know what people are talking about).

Branding as a main journalistic use was predicted by working at a digital-native news outlet (Table 3.2), indicating that self-promotion and cultivation of a public image belong mostly to the digital realm. In part, this could be related to perceptions of the digital-native startups as up-starts, without the reach and impact of legacy media. Digital journalists thus perhaps see social media as a way to validate their journalistic work—showcase the quality and credibility of their reporting, and ensure their stories are visible to as wide an audience as possible. Adding to this finding, the content analysis showed about 5% of sites' Instagram posts were dedicated to organizational branding.

Part of branding involves communicating with readers and receiving the public's feedback. Social media allow journalists at digital-native sites to get closer to their readers, and that close relationship is

Table 3.2 Factors predicting journalists' social media use for work

Journalist characteristics	Branding[a]		Reporting[b]		Monitoring the news[c]	
	Beta	p value	Beta	p value	Beta	p value
Gender	-.044	.363	.088	.095	-.076	.144
Age	.211	.000***	-.135	.013*	-.089	.096
Education	-.060	.217	.020	.708	.033	.523
Live in:						
Argentina	-.125	.159	.071	.466	.139	.143
Bolivia	.009	.871	-.035	.599	.075	.197
Brazil	-.038	.441	-.030	.577	-.057	.278
Colombia	-.095	.255	.036	.691	.028	.752
Costa Rica	-.020	.698	.016	.779	.040	.473
Cuba	-.029	.581	.011	.849	.030	.586
Dominican Republic	-.024	.694	-.062	.343	.075	.242
Ecuador	-.131	.078	.014	.863	.046	.561
El Salvador	.010	.870	-.070	.308	.041	.549
Guatemala	-.073	.313	.008	.919	.089	.249
Honduras	-.001	.990	-.007	.917	.102	.132
Mexico	-.035	.792	-.024	.868	.214	.130
Nicaragua	-.045	.480	-.072	.301	.166	.015*
Panama	-.050	.319	.048	.378	.077	.147
Paraguay	-.070	.164	.002	.971	.030	.569
Peru	-.061	.486	.020	.833	.114	.218
Puerto Rico	-.074	.148	-.037	.506	.057	.292

(Continued)

Table 3.2 (Continued)

Journalist characteristics	Branding[a] Beta	p value	Reporting[b] Beta	p value	Monitoring the news[c] Beta	p value
Uruguay	−.018	.736	−.047	.418	−.055	.330
Venezuela	−.164	.083	.052	.619	.204	.044*
Frequency of Facebook use for work	.059	.267	.013	.829	.166	.003**
Frequency of Twitter use for work	−.042	.420	.058	.304	.105	.057
Frequency of LinkedIn use for work	.024	.626	.032	.553	.014	.427
Frequency of YouTube use for work	−.009	.860	.093	.105	.044	.437
Frequency of Instagram use for work	.191	.000***	−.075	.216	.000	.996
Frequency of WhatsApp use for work	−.042	.410	.120	.030*	.068	.208
Database reporting	.121	.013*	.085	.107	−.003	.959
Social media for branding	–	–	.410	.000***	.224	.000***
Social media for reporting	.346	.000***	–	–	.117	.045*
Social media for monitoring the news	.197	.000***	.122	.045*	–	–
Importance of innovating technologically	.084	.100	−.014	.804	.155	.004**
Digital-native	.215	.000***	−.189	.001***	.004	.943
R^2	.445		.342		.366	
Adjusted R^2	.379***		.264***		.292	

Note: Living in Chile was the reference variable for country. Betas are standardized coefficients.

* $p < .05$,
** $p < .01$,
*** $p < .001$.
a [F(33, 279) = 6.774, $p < .001$].
b [F(33, 279) = 4.386, $p < .001$].
c [F(33, 279) = 4.890, $p < .001$].

fundamental to their identity as different than traditional, commercial media. As Ricardo from Mexico said during focus groups, "We define ourselves as a social media, not just as digital, because a very important part of our readers comes to us via social networks, and they don't just read, but also send comments, suggestions for topics, criticisms, and more. Interaction in social networks is a capital issue." Ávila said that unlike commercial media, which have massive yet less engaged audiences, "We're the opposite. We seek an audience that educates itself, we seek more quality time with the audience ... If we offer a lot to the audience, if we are loyal to the audience, they're going to participate and offer feedback and write and generate opinion."

While the digital-native journalists used social media for branding, it was the traditional journalists who used it for *reporting*. This could be because journalists at digital-native sites have innovated new ways of using technologies that assign a different meaning to reporting with social media, while traditional journalists have normalized social media for traditional reporting practices. It is easy to assume that social media reporting is tied to digital savviness, and it seems logical to associate such savviness with a publication born and raised online. However, to understand this finding, we need to keep in mind some of the fundamental content characteristic differences between digital-native sites and traditional media.

First, the digital-native sites focus on in-depth, explanatory, and investigative reporting—"slow journalism" that invokes different news values and alternative storytelling formats to emphasize quality, transparency, and long-form narratives (Le Masurier, 2015). Second, the digital-native outlets tend to have smaller newsrooms, meaning fewer reporters to cover breaking news. Third, these sites mostly focus on niche beats, like politics and corruption, human rights, or gender—they're not covering all the news of the day in the same way traditional, commercial media do. As such, journalists at digital-native sites have more time to cultivate expert and community sources, and so don't necessarily have to rely on social media to quickly find a source or report from the scene on deadline. Because they're not concerned with "feeding the beast" daily, they don't need social media as much to find story ideas to fill a news hole. In fact, less use of social media for reporting and more "boots on the ground" among digital-native journalists *should* be what we expect from reporters taking the time to go into the communities they cover, and find sources and stories and report on them in full, nuanced ways. Traditional journalists' reliance on social media for reporting perhaps speaks to the superficial coverage for which journalists from digital-native sites criticized them.

Monitoring the news, or using social media to keep up with breaking events and know what people are talking about, did not show significant differences between mainstream and digital-native journalists. This finding suggests staying on top of the news is a generic characteristic of journalists, regardless of where they work. This also provides evidence of digital-native outlets' orientations toward the professional, aligning them with the mainstream. It is not negative for the digital-native outlets to be like their traditional counterparts when it comes to valuing newsworthiness. However, just because both mainstream and digital-native outlets use social media to monitor the news does not mean they have the same conceptions of what news is important, or that they will cover it in the same ways. Monitoring the news was also predicted by being from Nicaragua or Venezuela. This country difference is worth highlighting, as it speaks to the importance of social media in countries where the government controls the press and limits freedom of expression, such as in Nicaragua and Venezuela. The start of this chapter called attention to the way Venezuela's *El Pitazo* uses social media as one of its principal tactics for circumventing the government's digital censorship. Social media thus become one of the only ways to monitor the news when independent outlets are censored, co-opted, or taken offline.

Social media's limitations

While the survey, interviews, and focus groups leave no doubt that journalists at digital-native sites see social media as an accepted part of their jobs, that's not to say they don't have reservations about using it. Throughout Latin America, journalists' uses of social media are limited by digital inequalities, misinformation, digital surveillance, threats, and defamation campaigns (Ganter & Paulino, 2021; Relly & González de Bustamante, 2014).

Many journalists at the digital-native outlets saw social media as creating unsafe spaces for journalists, both online and offline. "I think social networks give anyone the opportunity to feel entitled to insult you," *El Faro's* Carlos Dada said. Similarly, Mariona said that a lot of "feedback on social networks has been very violent … there's a lot of discrimination in comments." Journalists also noted that social media threats have real-world consequences, often manifested in offline attacks requiring physical protection. Outlets need to pay greater attention to their journalists' physical *and* mental health, journalists said, such as by providing counseling to help them manage the stress that comes not just from social media harassment, but from reporting generally. Carmen Riera of Venezuela said she was proud her outlet had provided group sessions with a psychologist, and she realized how uncommon it was. Most media, especially commercial media, "don't care a lot about people," she said, verbalizing these sites' disarticulation from the mainstream.

Overall, though, journalists from the digital-native sites saw value in social media. In part because of digital inequalities, social media help small digital-native sites gain influence and reach, which are necessary for sustainability. Recognizing the limits of being online in a country that, as of 2019, still only had an Internet penetration rate of 57% (Internet World Stats, 2021), Jose Luís Sanz, then-director of *El Faro*, noted,

> An outlet like *El Faro* is not commercially viable in El Salvador. If it were not for a platform like Facebook, we would not have made it. That was the only way to make it possible to be recognized even outside the country and show our journalistic quality.
>
> (Meléndez Yúdico, 2016, p. 18)

Social media also give the sites certain freedoms not possible in traditional media, allowing journalists to say things they normally wouldn't in a typical story. This is in line with previous research indicating journalists tend to break from traditional journalistic tenets of objectivity and distance when posting on social media (Borges-Rey, 2015; Lasorsa et al., 2012). Latin American journalists from digital-native sites said that because they are serving a different audience on social media, they can push more boundaries and showcase different perspectives. With more freedom on social media come more opportunities—and need—for innovation and creativity, they said. In this way, then, they're disrupting traditional journalism's normalization of social media. "In the way we talk, or converse, in what we publish, we're innovating on social media," Riera said.

Content analysis

To get at sites' innovation and creativity, this chapter content analyzed[2] Instagram posts from eight digital-native news sites in four South American countries: Ecuador's *BN Periodismo* and *Primicias*, Colombia's *La Silla Vacía* and *La Oreja Roja*, Chile's *CIPER* and *The Clinic*, and Venezuela's *Efecto Cocuyo* and *El Pitazo*. All eight sites are included in SembraMedia's directory of independent, digital-native media.

The *heterodox-creative logic* (Mowbray, 2015), which emphasizes alternative media's creativity, innovation, and aesthetic form as critical tools for disrupting hegemonic, commercial media, stems from the "fusion of art and activism" (Hamilton, 2009, p. 175). This "aestheticization of dissent" (Hamilton, 2009, p. 161) entails the "adding, editing, or otherwise recontextualizing" of commercial artifacts to critique "not only dominant modes of production ... but dominant social conventions and relations of capitalism and other cultures of oppression" (Hamilton, 2009, p. 176). Through a lens of the heterodox-creative logics of alternative media, this content analysis sheds light on the creative tactics employed on the sites' social media accounts to understand how these sites are innovating in content, in interactivity, and in discourse, reflecting and challenging mainstream journalism.

Rhetorical creativity to subvert the status quo emerged in the content analysis as a main Instagram tactic: more posts took a bottom-up approach (38%) that showcased ordinary citizens' perspectives, than the top-down perspective (25%) typical of mainstream news. Disrupting the traditional journalist-audience relationship, more than half of posts mentioned readers, and of those, about 97% talked directly to them. Topics also contested the mainstream: about 63% of posts were related to a social justice issue, and nearly a quarter of posts overtly took a stance—of those, about 17% were in opposition to the government. When activists or protesters were mentioned, most posts (81.1%) depicted them in positive or legitimizing ways, 16.4% were neutral, and 2.5% were negative or delegitimizing. In contrast, of the posts that mentioned government or ruling elites, 36.7% portrayed them negatively, 63% were neutral, and a mere .3% were positive.

These findings point to the sites' alternative-oriented focus on citizens over elites and authorities. While protesters and social movements often are depicted negatively in mainstream news coverage when they challenge the status quo (McLeod & Hertog, 1999), Instagram offers these digital-native news sites a space to showcase activists' causes and actions, and to do so in non-delegitimizing ways. News coverage of protests shared on social media tends to be more favorable than that published overall in newspapers (Harlow & Kilgo, 2021), so by highlighting social justice posts and taking anti-status quo perspectives that elevate ordinary citizens and protesters over ruling authorities, these sites in effect used social media to challenge hegemonic media and political power.

Country comparisons

The four countries included in this study share important commonalities in their media systems, such as concentration, commercialism, and a weak public interest. Still, it is imperative to recognize their differences. For example, starting with the 1998 election of Hugo Chávez as Venezuela's president, Latin American countries like Venezuela, Chile, and Ecuador began a turn toward the left and radical social democracy as part of the so-called "pink tide" (Artz, 2017). In contrast, Colombia maintained its conservative bent and close ties with the United States. While the mid-2010s saw a conservative backlash that mostly swept out the leftists, in 2019 we began seeing a resurgence of the left, such as with anti-government and anti-police brutality protests in Colombia, anti-austerity protests in Ecuador, and protests related to inequality stemming from neo-liberalism in Chile. In Venezuela, Chávez's Bolivarian revolution collapsed into a political, economic, and humanitarian crisis. These political and economic factors are key to press freedom, considered "problematic" in Chile and Ecuador, and "bad" in Colombia and Venezuela, according to Reporters Without Borders' 2021 World Press Freedom Index.

The content analysis highlights important cross-country differences (Table 3.3). In Colombia, where citizens, tired of decades of seemingly never-ending armed conflict, have been protesting and journalists, often threatened and hamstrung by media owners' clientelist ties with political and economic classes, are migrating from traditional to digital-native outlets, post hoc Tukey tests showed more posts written from the bottom-up/citizens' perspective or that took a stance than in any of the other three countries. Additionally, Colombian outlets posted more about human rights, media reform, and press freedom than other countries, and less about arts/entertainment/science/sports, reflecting journalists' and citizens' lived realities. Human rights violations during the war, a return to security policies that previously resulted in human rights violations, and, following the government's failures during the peace process with the FARC guerrillas, an increase in violence against social leaders and ex-combatants, all explain why Colombian journalists might be more concerned with human rights stories. In contrast, Colombian posts mentioned and spoke directly to readers significantly less than did posts from the other countries, which could signal less importance placed on audience interaction and more of a traditional journalistic approach to audience relations. For the other countries, though, talking to readers could be a way to create a sense of community, and get closer to readers, articulating them more

Table 3.3 Comparison of Instagram content, by country

Post characteristics	Chile	Colombia	Ecuador	Venezuela	F score (d.f.)
Ordinary citizens' perspective	.33 (.47)	.52 (.50)	.15 (.36)	.33 (.47)	F(3, 651) = 6.422***
Takes a stance	.16 (.37)	.51 (.50)	.09 (.29)	.12 (.33)	F(3, 651) = 21.110***
Mentions investigative reporting	.02 (.14)	.03 (.18)	.00 (.00)	.01 (.08)	F(3, 651) = 1.703
Educational	.08 (.27)	.07 (.25)	.09 (.29)	.12 (.32)	F(3, 651) = 1.013
Mentions readers	.96 (.16)	.87 (.34)	.95 (.23)	.98 (.31)	F(3, 651) = 7.46***
Talks directly to readers	.99 (.10)	.85 (.36)	.96 (.19)	.99 (.11)	F(3, 651) = 14.340***
Uses hashtags	.78 (.42)	.80 (.40)	.55 (.50)	.95 (.22)	F(3, 651) = 27.872***
Uses emojis	.91 (.28)	.34 (.48)	.20 (.40)	.11 (.31)	F(3, 651) = 252.518***
Uses GIFs	.01 (.07)	.00 (.00)	.00 (.00)	.11 (.31)	F(3, 1212) = .786
Uses infographics	.84 (.37)	.64 (.48)	.67 (.47)	.45 (.50)	F(3, 651) = 31.125***
Uses photos or videos	.42 (.16)	.39 (.13)	.43 (.17)	.39 (.13)	F(3, 651) = 2.630*
Ordinary voices sourced	.09 (.29)	.05 (.22)	.07 (.26)	.06 (.23)	F(3, 1212) = 1.029
Mobilizing	.08 (.23)	.11 (.23)	.14 (.28)	.39 (.13)	F(3, 1212) = .971
Topic: gender/LGBTQ	.05 (.22)	.02 (.13)	.00 (.00)	.04 (.19)	F(3, 1212) = 1.332
Media reform	.00 (.00)	.07 (.25)	.00 (.00)	.02 (.14)	F(3, 1212) = 4.506**
Human rights	.05 (.15)	.11 (.20)	.03 (.12)	.07 (.17)	F(3, 1212) = 7.37***
Arts/science/entertainment/sports	.16 (.37)	.02 (.13)	.18 (.39)	.11 (.31)	F(3, 1212) = 3.943**
Organizational branding	.09 (.29)	.05 (.22)	.13 (.34)	.06 (.23)	F(3, 1212) = 1.697
Government/politics	.22 (.42)	.28 (.45)	.25 (.44)	.17 (.38)	F(3, 1212) = 1.851
Economics/labor/education	.11 (.32)	.10 (.30)	.00 (.00)	.10 (.30)	F(3, 1212) = 2.209
Environment/weather	.05 (.22)	.02 (.13)	.05 (.23)	.09 (.29)	F(3, 1212) = 2.251
Health	.21 (.40)	.33 (.47)	.29 (.46)	.25 (.44)	F(3, 1212) = 1.529

Note: All post characteristics were measured dichotomously, where 0 = not present and 1 = present. Values represent means with standard deviations in parentheses.

* p < .05,
** p < .01,
*** p < .001.

toward the alternative. These findings reinforce the notion that not all independent, digital-native sites are created equal, and their social media articulations toward the mainstream or alternative can vary based on outlet- and country contextualities.

Hashtags, emojis

The eight sites' use of hashtags, emojis, GIFs, and other multimedia elements can be seen as a recontextualization of the traditional journalist-audience relationship, and thus a critique of the mainstream, in line with the heterodox-creative logics of alternative media. About 76.7% of posts included hashtags, 29.2% used emojis, .2% included GIFs, 51% had infographics, 20% included videos, 80.7% included a photo, and 18.4% offered a photo gallery. The presence of hashtags and use of emojis were positively correlated with Instagram posts that mentioned readers or talked directly to them. This speaks to the role of hashtags and emojis as rhetorical devices to signal shared emotions and to construct community (Bennett & Segerberg, 2013; Enli & Simonsen, 2018).

Emotional content on social media increases overall user engagement (Berger & Milkman, 2012), and results here showed sites' use of emojis was related to an increase in the number of likes and comments a post received. Importantly, emojis were also associated with posts that were mobilizing and that included ordinary voices as sources. This suggests that not only might emojis be involved in the creation of community generally but also potentially in the creation of networked counter publics, and even activist publics coming together on Instagram via calls to action and posts with mobilizing information. At the same time, however, the content analysis showed that hashtags and emojis were negatively correlated with posts that took a stance, or that mentioned social justice or human rights. This doesn't necessarily contradict the notion of their contribution to community and counter- and activist-publics. Rather, it points to sites' articulation with the professional to balance out any inclination toward activism that might somehow discredit them and create controversy overshadowing the importance of a social justice or human rights-related story.

Sites' choice of emojis also is noteworthy. Most common were illustrative uses of emojis: icons of video cameras to signal the presence of a video, or pointing finger and arrow emojis used to draw attention to something, like a link. These uses of emojis are fairly common and don't stray from what have come to be recognized as typical ways of marking text on social media. Sites also got creative with emojis to illustrate text, such as a money bag emoji used in posts about government corruption, the yellow triangle hazard warning sign used to fact-check false claims, or a palm tree and beach umbrella in a post about vacations. Such use fits with research suggesting that emojis can be used to clarify or emphasize textual information, thus reducing any misunderstandings (Riordan & Glikson, 2020).

These sites also employed emojis to go beyond illustrating their reporting, using them to express emotions and opinions about the news, representing a break with traditional journalistic norms about objectivity. For example, *The Clinic* posted a sad-face emoji in a post about tourists flocking to the beach amid a pandemic. *La Oreja Roja* also used the sad-face emoji in a post that expressed displeasure with the Colombian president, comparing his administration to that of the Chilean dictatorship of Pinochet. *La Silla Vacía* used the mind-blown emoji in posts about rising poverty and the increasing number of COVID cases.

Such affective use of emojis to emotionally connect with readers strengthens research from outside the Global South that indicates digital journalists are taking on more of an interventionist role online (Ferrucci & Vos 2017; Haim et al., 2021). Journalists' professional posts have been shown to reflect rhetorical practices of ordinary users, thus challenging the journalistic norm of objectivity (Hågvar, 2019; Welbers & Opgenhaffen, 2019). Overall, by taking stances and using emojis to express opinion and emotion, this content analysis showed that sites' interventionist roles represent a clear disarticulation from traditional, mainstream media, where editorial agendas are hidden behind the façade of objectivity. At the same time, though, sites' limited use of emojis when it came to social-justice-related posts and stance-taking point to a professional orientation, thus accentuating the often-conflicting articulations of diverse social media practices at these digital-native outlets.

Audience interaction

This content analysis also adds to "shareworthiness" (Trilling et al., 2017) scholarship, showing that the presence of emojis, GIFs, and infographics on the eight South American sites' Instagram pages was positively correlated with the number of likes and comments a post received (Table 3.4). Previous research points to news values, post topic and length, controversial content, and clickbait headlines (Heiss et al., 2019; Kuiken, et al., 2017; Tenenboim, & Cohen, 2015; Trilling et al., 2017) as influencing interaction on social media. Country and type of news outlet, presence of multimedia features, and framing of news stories also relate to interaction (García-Perdomo et al., 2018;

Table 3.4 Predictors of Instagram interactions

Outlet/post characteristics	Likes[a] Beta	p value	Comments[b] Beta	p value
Outlet country:				
Chile	.455	.000***	.383	.000***
Colombia	.286	.000***	.070	.051
Ecuador	−.044	.156	−.068	.034*
Written from ordinary citizens' perspective	−.051	.094	−.033	.304
Takes a stance	−.026	.447	−.083	.019*
Citizen sources dominant	.047	.091	−.004	.890
Includes mobilizing information	−.058	.036*	−.031	.277
Educational	−.053	.046*	−.054	.052
Post topic:				
Gender/LGBTQ+	−.022	.460	.060	.050
Immigration	−.028	.318	.005	.865
Media reform/freedom of expression	.025	.353	.052	.069
General human rights	−.051	.163	.008	.832
Organizational branding	−.033	.293	−.016	.617
Politics/government	−.043	.283	.116	.006**
Economy/education	−.103	.002**	−.017	.613
Environment	−.047	.134	−.025	.435
Health	−.126	.002**	−.035	.399
Other	.025	.380	.069	.020*
Includes hashtags	.058	.042*	.060	.043*
Includes emojis	−.065	.040*	−.033	.317
Includes GIFs	.105	.000***	.114	.000***
Includes infographics	.082	.004**	.081	.007**
Includes photos/videos	.079	.002**	.001	.966
R^2	.268		.208	
Adjusted R^2	.253***		.192***	

Note: Venezuela and posts about arts/science/entertainment/sports were reference variables. Betas are standardized coefficients.

* $p < .05$,
** $p < .01$,
*** $p < .001$.
a [$F(23, 1179) = 18.73, p < .001$].
b [$F(23, 1179) = 13.44, p < .001$].

Harlow & Kilgo, 2021; Harlow et al., 2017, 2020). Given that Instagram is the social platform dedicated to visuals, and we have long recognized the power of visuals for drawing audiences' attention and eliciting emotions, it is important to consider how news organizations can use the affordances of Instagram for improving audience interaction. Further, just as the moving images of television created a "kind of synchronous viewing solidarity" during the Civil Rights Movement in the United States in the 1960s (Richardson, 2020, p. 36), it is worth considering how news on Instagram might contribute to a new, *socially shared solidarity* facilitated by independent, digital-native news sites.

Results showed users interacted differently depending on the post topic. Posts about heavier topics like economic inequality or health during a global pandemic prompted fewer likes than posts about arts/science/entertainment/sports—in other words, light or feature stories were associated with likes, or "light" engagement. More substantial engagement, though, like comments, showed the opposite: "heavier" topics like politics and government corruption prompted more comments than posts about arts/science/entertainment/sports. Many of the countries under study here are dealing with high levels of corruption often ignored in traditional media, leaving the digital-native sites as one of the only places for audiences to inform themselves or have debates. Practically, these findings have important consequences for digital-native outlets seeking to build community and encourage user participation.

It was somewhat of a surprise to see that posts with more of an activist or alternative orientation, such as those that were educational or mobilizing, prompted fewer likes, and stance-taking predicted fewer comments, even though correlations showed stance-taking was associated with more likes (t = .102, p < .001). One optimistic explanation, perhaps, is that fewer likes for the educational and mobilizing posts meant these posts in fact educated and mobilized users, driving them to the news sites' main pages to read the full story. However, it is likely that these posts were just not as engaging for users, simply because they did not include the hashtags and emojis that are necessary for more interaction. The fact that fewer comments were predicted by posts that took a stance could be related to the audiences' affinity with these sites. Stance-taking was correlated with likes, indicating that audiences approved of the positions the outlets held, thereby potentially precluding any need for them to comment. If users agree with the stance, liking the post seems to make more sense than posting a comment saying they agree.

Combined, these findings about sites' affective emoji uses and posts' "shareworthiness" indicate that a more interventionist journalism on social media—especially when it comes to social justice issues—that takes advantage of emojis and other multimedia features could garner more audience interaction. This suggests that following the heterodox-creative logics of alternative media, and resisting mainstream media's normalized uses of social media, could ultimately bring these sites the user interaction they seek in their quests for sustainability.

Conclusion

The content analysis, combined with the survey, focus groups, and interviews, all point to the heterogeneity of social media in journalism. Journalists not only innovated in how they used social media in their work, but their responses to digital violence also suggest innovation and a break with traditional media, such as in their approach to mental health and security. The innovativeness of digital-native sites also came through on Instagram, as the sites' posts can be seen as a recontextualization and critique of traditional, mainstream media and its normalization of social media. Their use of emojis and multimedia, and the way they focused on grassroots perspectives and openly took stances, illustrated that Mowbray's (2015) concept of the heterodox-creative logics of alternative media can be applied to sites' social media practices, creating a heterodox-creative logic of digital-native news. For these independent, digital-native news sites, social media represented less of a normalization of traditional journalistic practices, and more of an adoption of non-normative behaviors (Falck & Barnes, 1975): rather than rejecting or adopting prevailing norms about what the journalist-audience relationship should look like or whether or not positionality should be made transparent, these sites instead proposed something new. Instead of sticking to the status quo (normative behaviors) and changing nothing, or entirely rejecting the dominant norms (deviant behavior) and having any potential changes shot down via hegemony, these site's non-normative behaviors perhaps represent an opening for structural changes when it comes to the role of social media in journalism. Sites' affective use of emojis, stance-taking, and bottom-up and oppositional posts are disrupting traditional journalistic norms and practices, influencing audience interaction and potentially contributing to a socially shared solidarity. Thus, when it comes to social media, such non-normative behaviors and disarticulations from traditional media point to the sites as change agents, with important consequences for the heterodox potential of social media in journalism.

Notes

1 http://www.sembramedia.org/sembramedia-directory/
2 The content analysis included a stratified random sample of 1,216 Instagram posts from eight independent, digital-native news sites published from March 2020 through March 2021, with posts sampled according to publication and

time of day they were posted. Post links and their accompanying social interaction data were collected using Facebook's CrowdTangle, a social media monitoring tool that tracks public interaction data (likes, comments, shares, reactions). About 30.2% of posts came from *Efecto Cocuyo*, 16% from *El Pitazo*, 15.9% from *La Oreja Roja*, 12.7% from *The Clinic*, 9.5% from *Primicias*, 5.5% from *BN Periodismo*, and 4% each from *La Silla Vacía* and *CIPER*. Posts were primarily coded by one paid coder. Inter-coder reliability was calculated on 10% of the sample, resulting in the following Krippendorff's alpha scores: .79 (official sources), .81 (activist sources), .88 (post written from a top-down perspective typical of traditional news stories), .83 (post written from a bottom-up, grassroots perspective of ordinary citizens), 1 (post takes a stance), 1 (post about activist issues), .89 (topic of post), .97 (depiction of protesters), 1 (post includes mobilizing information), 1 (post includes a call to action), .93 (post is educational), 1 (post is about an investigative story), .93 (post speaks directly to readers), 1 (post promotes site/content/organizational branding), 1 (post includes a hashtag), 1 (post includes a photo or video), 1 (post includes emojis), 1 (post includes a GIF), .93 (post includes an infographic), and 1 (post includes a link).

4 Journalism with a Feminist Gaze

Argentina's female-led and gender-focused news site *La Nota* arose from the recognition that certain perspectives—namely, those related to feminist or LGBTQ+ agendas—were mostly absent from the traditional, market-oriented mainstream media of the conservative province of Tucumán in the country's northwest. Acknowledging, though, the limits of alternative media for reaching broad audiences and contesting powerful, hegemonic media, *La Nota* set out to try to mainstream a human rights agenda and feminist perspectives.

"We're not interested in being an alternative medium," said *La Nota* founder Milagro Mariona when I interviewed her in 2021. Instead, she said, they want to capture the audiences of corporate media, and challenge those outlets' domination of the mediasphere. Plus, she said, "alternative" is looked at pejoratively, and in today's diverse, digital landscape, the term itself has lost meaning and become obsolete.

That doesn't mean, though, that *La Nota* isn't providing a much-needed alternative to mainstream media and its allegiances to the status quo and economic and political elites. Most of *La Nota's* journalists come from an alternative media background or have been connected to feminist movements. In fact, the site has created a space for the intersection of journalism and militancy, Mariona said, and makes clear its feminist stance and anti-hegemonic agenda. "From a gender and human rights perspective, we address issues of a different nature," the site says on its Facebook page. In *La Nota*, Mariona said, "we *militate* [fight for a belief]."

La Nota is just one of dozens of such independent, *cause-based* digital-native sites in Latin America doing journalism with a feminist or gender-focused lens. "Today we have a lot of media that, in addition to being started and directed by women, also make a commitment to an epistemological change by calling themselves feminist journalists or feminist media," said Isabel González, an Ecuadorian ambassador

DOI: 10.4324/9781003152477-4

of Chicas Poderosas, a Latin American network of women journalists working to close the gender gap in media (Estarque, 2020).

An estimated 40% of independent, digital-native news sites in Latin America are founded or directed by women (SembraMedia, 2017). By comparison, only about 15% of such startups in Europe are founded by women (Kollmann et al., 2016), and overall, only about 20% of global startups in 2019 were founded by women (Crunchbase, 2020).

For the women news site founders and journalists I interviewed, going digital gave them the freedom to pursue the feminist and human rights agendas they saw as important, but also allowed them to experiment with innovative approaches to journalistic norms and practices, unencumbered by the patriarchy and sexism of traditional media. Based on interviews with founders and journalists, this chapter shows journalism with a feminist gaze influences everything from why these sites were launched, their news content, and reporting practices, to the composition of their teams, the business models they employ, and the trainings they conduct to influence where journalism is headed. This feminist gaze orients these sites toward activism as well as professional journalism, while still demarcating them from traditional, mainstream media.

Contesting the hegemony of "macho media"

If you're a woman journalist in Latin America, "you're probably not working in what feels like a safe space," said Belén Arce Teceros, communications director for Chicas Poderosas. Top-down, patriarchal dynamics at most mainstream outlets don't allow women to cover the news in the way they want, she said. "A lot of the voices are not being represented ... Many topics and conversations are not being heard in the media."

News media, and news itself, have been conceptualized as masculine constructs, reflecting men's hegemonic ways of thinking about what is important or relevant (Bachmann, 2020). Newsworthiness and professional norms and practices have developed around men's standards (Carter et al., 2019; Harp, 2007), ultimately marginalizing women and relegating their voices and concerns to women's pages, limiting women to the private sphere and "soft" news (North, 2016). News media reinforce patriarchy and the status quo through content that ultimately serves to "keep women in their proper place" (Bachmann, 2020, p. 3). Even objectivity and impartiality as news values have been critiqued for reflecting patriarchal hegemony (Carter et al., 2019).

In interviews, journalists described the gender-focused, digital-native sites as in resistance to such patriarchal, sexist narratives. Refusing to be limited to women's pages and bound to the private sphere of home and family, these women journalists broke out of the so-called "malestream" media to create their own spaces, pioneering feminist approaches that re-center news values and practices around innovative non-hegemonic, non-patriarchal, non-heteronormative understandings of journalism.

"We're in a good moment," Arce Teceros said, because a lot of independent, digital-native and feminist media outlets, alongside organizations and social movements, "are helping start other conversations and bring these topics to the table and make them visible not only in the media, but to society at large."

Filling an unmet need

In traditional outlets, there's still a disdain for news that is seen as specific to women, which is contributing to the growth of digital-native sites with feminist perspectives, journalists said. Interviews revealed that these sites were created to fill an unmet need: women journalists realized there was no space in traditional media for the kind of journalism they believed needed to be done, so they started creating their own outlets. "We women are 50% or more of the population, so our issues should be covered universally, but in practice they're not. There persists this narrative that they're minority or niche issues," said Laura Aguirre, co-founder of a feminist news site in El Salvador. Digital-native outlets are a reaction against this, she said, citing her own outlet, *Alharaca*, as an example.

Alharaca was born from the exhaustion and frustration of fighting for space for feminist reporting. The site developed from a multimedia news project about reproductive health, Sexo Sinvergüenzas (Sex Scoundrels, a name that doubles as a play on words implying sex without shame), that they had trouble finding a home to publish, in part because it had received a grant from Planned Parenthood Global. Not only were outlets reluctant to publish the topic, they also didn't want to run anything with funding from an organization that supported abortion, because they worried it could damage their credibility and objectivity, the sites' founders said. "It motivated us to decide to do something on our own, that would have our values, and where we could do what we wanted without asking anyone," said Jimena Aguilar, one of the site's founders.

In 2019 *Alharaca* launched as an independent, feminist medium. The name, which roughly translates as "fuss," is a derogatory term used to describe people (usually women) who make a lot of noise about nothing important. They decided to re-appropriate the word and use it against their critics. "It's a phrase that has been heard said ... about women who do journalism focused on gender issues, and that's how we decided to retake the word and change its meaning a little—or a lot," Aguilar said.

Honduras' *ContraCorriente* similarly started out of discontent. "We're feminists, and we wanted to tell the stories that we know are told so badly, and we come from spaces where we've seen how the media are telling these destructive narratives," co-founder Jennifer Ávila said. "Women have grown tired of newsrooms where there's no equity, where there's a lot of sexism, where they can't advance unless they continue covering culture or showbusiness ... They're just fed up with traditional newsrooms."

The experiences of these journalists echo those of women around the world: "women's invisibility as subjects and sources in the news is still the norm especially for marginalized women," according to the Global Media Monitoring Project (GMMP, 2021a), which includes 16 Latin American countries. The July 2021 GMMP (2021b) report showed that while about 35% of reporters in Latin America are women, gender-related stories comprise less than 3% of the traditional news media's agenda. The report noted a "loss in the quality of stories from a gender perspective ... News stories are as unlikely to clearly challenge gender stereotypes today as they were 15 years ago." Across Latin America, women were included as subjects or sources in about 26% of coverage, and women were presented in familial terms three times more than men—when women were quoted, most were sex workers or housewives. Such sourcing practices contribute to the divide between women in private spheres and men in public ones—only 11% of stories included women as expert sources.

Just as news sites focused on gender and human rights have been motivated by the failings of mainstream media, they've been enabled by the changing social and political climate, journalists said. Research shows independent, digital news sites, more than traditional media, have been foundational for the success of various gender-related social movements in Latin America in recent years (Martínez, 2018). Arce Teceros explained that massive citizen mobilization efforts against femicide have

> opened the door for other thoughts regarding feminism that used to be super leftist and super radical and like, oh, you're crazy because you have these ideas. It's much more mainstream now ... All these changes have opened up new ideas and debates related to a different way of telling stories, and that's related to this gender perspective or rights perspective.

Similarly, Aguilar said,

> Before there were no media led only by women. But now there's more opportunity for success, in the sense that new generations no longer take for granted that change is necessary; feminist movements are happening throughout Latin America. It's like a wave that's gaining strength in all Latin America and I think audiences don't want to hear just the same perspective from the same fifty-year-old guys. They want to hear other opinions, see themselves reflected. We see this more and more from women working in journalism. They're more willing to confront their bosses without fear of repercussion.

Sometimes that means leaving, and starting their own sites to be able to publish the gender-related stories traditional outlets won't. "I think we were the first to do it (in El Salvador), but we're not the last," Aguilar said.

Feminist reporting norms

Creating their own sites has allowed these journalists to report news in a way that breaks the macho media mold. Interviews showed that these gender-focused sites practiced a different way of telling stories where they saw journalism as activism, evident not just when it came to gatekeeping and their definitions of newsworthiness, but also in their sourcing practices, word choices, and the ethics and norms they followed. Part of being a feminist journalist means not just reporting on drama or tragedies, like other media do, but "proposing a new narrative to tell a different story," Mariona said. Importantly, these narratives are not necessarily neutral or judgment-free in the traditional journalistic way. "I can be objective, but that doesn't mean losing my subjectivity as a woman, as a lesbian, as someone from Tucumán," she said. "And that [subjectivity] doesn't mean the information isn't real or truthful."

For these journalists, objectivity in the face of injustice was seen as an outdated, falsely idealistic way of doing journalism that ultimately did readers a disservice. "Journalism can defend human rights," Isabela Ponce, co-founder of *GK* in Ecuador, said, adding that most mainstream, corporate media don't focus on gender or human rights because they're worried about "losing their credibility or objectivity, as if that were possible. It's an old-school way of thinking. Taking a stand and defending a cause isn't bad, but they've been trained as if it were something bad." Journalists have a responsibility to defend human rights and justice, she said, because "they have the power to be able to change ideas and prejudices through data" with journalism that is still "rigorous" and "in-depth," as good journalism should be. There's a rise in independent, digital-native sites focused on gender and human rights, she said, precisely because the young journalists—women—who are founding these sites are "tired of the traditional structures, of this idea of objectivity. The world is going at a different pace, with other realities, and journalism is changing." Likewise, Aguilar said that objectivity, which she defined as the idea that your own prejudices and experiences don't affect you or your work as a journalist, is an "antiquated" idea. "The only thing we can do is be honest about our filters, and that obviously, gender equality is important to us," she said. And that means sometimes taking a position. "For us, it's not debatable that we have to respect and comply with the rights of women, and to monitor the factions of power that are supposed to make sure they're complied with and respected," Aguilar said.

Such undebatability of gender and human rights isn't about doing activism per se, but doing a justice-centered journalism—*real* journalism. Taking a feminist stance means "we don't make a division between activism, feminism, and journalism," Aguirre said.

> We are a feminist medium that responds to certain ethical principles that should be applied to coverage, in publications, in the way we represent people ... We have no aspiration to neutrality nor impartiality. In fact, it's the total opposite; we are absolutely partial ... We have an aspiration to tell the truth; we're in favor of the truth ... We separate ourselves from the mainstream ideas about journalism.

Mainstream media's contention that impartiality is possible is "wrong," she said. All journalists' representations of reality are partial because that vision is filtered through

> your gender, your social class position, your ethnicity, etcetera etcetera. And those things are never discussed in a traditional medium ... I believe that feminist ethics allows you to do a more honest, more authentic journalism, without the limitations of traditional journalistic practices. I am doing activism with journalistic methods. We follow the traditional journalistic methods of evidence, sources, investigations, *plus* feminist principles.

These journalists' critiques of mainstream media's objectivity and impartiality are important to recognize for the way they contest the male-centric notion of neutrality as a normative ideal. Their stance-taking and feminist positionality don't make their reporting less professional or credible, but more *honest*, as the journalists said. A gender- or human rights gaze thus represents these sites' innovative take on journalistic norms, ethics, roles, and responsibilities, and the belief that journalism must be proactive in improving the way it serves women and LGBTQ+ communities.

Feminist sourcing, reporting

Most of the journalists said their outlets have some kind of ethical or editorial policy, based on feminist perspectives, that addresses how to report stories so they don't follow the misogynistic patterns of most traditional media. Those same principles also ensure they adhere to professional journalism practices, like verification and balance. For these journalists, doing professional journalism does not preclude—in fact, it requires—a gender perspective. *ContraCorriente*, for example, tries to ensure gender parity in its sourcing. Most media tend to interview men as experts, even if the story topic is women survivors of violence, Ávila said, so "we make an effort to look for voices of professional women that can talk about these issues ... I'm not saying we don't interview men, but we try to look for more equilibrium of voices." Similarly, Ponce pointed out the importance of interviewing women, and not just men, for articles about the economy, science, or technology—"hard" news. The lack of sourcing equality is what led Carmen Riera to co-found Mujeres Referentes, an online database for Venezuelan journalists with contact information of women and non-binary experts. The idea, Riera said, is to help journalists "utilize and amplify other voices and be more pluralistic in their stories. Because the majority of people in our phone books? They're men."

    A feminist gaze influences not just who is quoted, but how their stories are told. When journalists leave traditional, commercial media to create digital outlets, they have the chance to "design editorial lines that are respectful of human rights," said Luz Mely Reyes, founder of Venezuela's *Efecto Cocuyo*. "Media have to be conscious of the way they represent groups, women, homosexual people, lesbians, Black people ... We can't disregard this responsibility." Her point is well taken, as it speaks to the differences in how gender is understood across cultures and across the globe (Bachmann & Proust, 2020). When media refer to women generally, it can sometimes obscure the heterogeneity in women's experiences with reproductive health, education, violence, or labor rights, for example. These digital sites' efforts toward gender equality in reporting practices and news product thus must also consider the nature of gender divides and the lack of uniformity in how gender is experienced.

Interviewees suggested reporting with such an ethos requires different practices that involve getting close to the people they're writing about, being accountable to them, and avoiding (re)inflicting trauma, in line with the praxis of intersectional journalism (Peterson-Salahuddin, 2021). For example, when writing about vulnerable populations, the LGBTQ+ community, or women in violent situations, they have to make sure their representations correspond with how the subjects see themselves, and not how the journalist imagines the subjects see themselves, which "is very different" from what other media do, Aguirre said. A true gender focus is not covering gender with a traditional, patriarchal journalistic lens, but rather explaining different inequalities and intersectionality when it comes to oppressions related to gender, social class, ethnicity, or ability, she said. It requires letting people share their perspectives, which goes beyond merely reporting facts. It's about explaining the systemic failures, and not just focusing on one extreme case that ultimately serves to re-victimize people, she said. This is especially important considering the GMMP (2021b) report found that coverage of violence against women was revictimizing, lacked a gender perspective, and failed to address solutions. At *ContraCorriente*, Ávila said, "we have a preference for a certain type of journalist that can write about femicide and sexual violence, not because they have better training, but because they do better at getting close to the victims to tell their stories." *Efecto Cocuyo* also has made efforts to get close to the communities it covers, such as with coffee shop meetings with feminist organizations in various cities to discuss how the outlet could improve its coverage, and to design an awareness campaign around a gender agenda.

For these journalists, adopting a gender perspective also involves being conscious of the importance of word choice. It can be something as small as naming the wife of someone, instead of just referring to her as the spouse, Ponce said. Aguirre said she sees language as a political tool. So when journalists at *Alharaca* use an "X" at the end of certain nouns to avoid using masculine or feminine endings, "the X makes it very clear what our political position is," Aguirre said. Other outlets' style guidelines for using inclusive language aren't necessarily about making words gender-neutral, but rather using language that centers women or someone from the LGBTQ+ community. For example, journalists defend human rights by the language they use, Riera said, such as making the decision, when police shoot someone, to use the word "kill," not "take down," or not to refer to femicide as a "crime of passion," a phrase journalists repeatedly condemned in interviews for the way it excused men when they murdered women.

Business models, organizational structures, and a transformed work culture

Just as these sites innovate reporting practices to center gender rights and feminism, interviews also revealed the way a gender perspective permeates these sites' business models, affecting who they hire, how they're funded, and how decisions are made.

Most of the teams working at these sites are comprised nearly entirely of women, working at all levels of the organization. *GK* has been conscientious about hiring women for leadership positions that normally are occupied by men, Ponce said. A focus on gender and equality in the news "obviously requires the presence and brains of women," she said. *ContraCorriente's* staff is comprised of 11 women (including the founders and two administrative assistants), and four men. Having women leaders means "women [employees] feel more confident that we're going to support them no matter what," Ávila said. For example, several of their female journalists have been sexually harassed by sources, so the outlet has created protocols to deal with such situations, making the outlet more appealing for women to want to work there. When they see there's a gender policy that has been institutionalized, and that the directors are women who are going to speak up in favor of women, it creates a safer space all around, Ávila said, because "the men are very, very cautious about what they say because they don't want to lose their job ... They understand they can't go around doing what before they thought was normal, and I think that's good." Chicas Poderosas fosters and promotes a different approach to labor relations in news media, Arce Teceros said, through

> collaborative journalism and practices that are based more on a feminist approach or caring for each other with a human approach. And that's really not often seen in the media, especially because of the dynamics of organizations. So, I think we create these spaces that we try to make them safe, and we try to make these spaces environments for learning and for asking questions and for not feeling afraid.

Just as a gender or feminist gaze influences hiring practices, it also impacts funding. As evidenced by *Alharaca's* trouble finding a home for the Sexo Sinvergüenzas project, journalism with a feminist perspective can potentially alienate advertisers and some readers, requiring these sites to innovate in financing options and business models. Most of the sites rely heavily on grants and international foundation funding. One of *Alharaca's* primary revenue streams involves offering consulting services, such as organizing events or designing communication campaigns or websites for organizations. "The value component of our business model is that we are specialists in gender issues, in diversity. That is a component that other advertising agencies or media do not have," Aguirre said. *ContraCorriente* also offers communication services—mostly to businesses or organizations working with women—teaching groups how to use social media or conduct a campaign. Doing so helps women, while also keeping *ContraCorriente* in business, Ávila said.

Being free from the constraints that come with commercial advertising allows these sites to establish horizontal organizational structures and pursue labor practices that reflect a feminist ethic. Entrepreneurship generally tends to be seen as "manly" (Gupta et al., 2009), and media entrepreneurship is associated with men (Geertsema-Sligh, 2014), underscoring the need for more women entrepreneurs in media in order to "expand the gender approach" and create exemplars for other women to follow, because "we have to look for our own model of leadership," Reyes said. She said,

> We all know there's a patriarchal leadership model. We all know that media are not especially a place for a lot of democracy or a lot of freedom, because they're vertical structures; they respond more to corporate structures. But we also know that there is a space for discussion, conversation. So what also makes us different, what we do differently, is we seek horizontal decision-making. And we also try to identify the patriarchal biases that we may have due to our training.

Safety and mental health

A gender perspective also relates to security and how outlets take care of their journalists, especially when it comes to self-care and mental health, interviews showed. "They are trying to change their practices and to be more human, basically, and to check in more with their people ... . It's not only telling the story about a trans woman or about abortion, it's also about changing the practices within the newsroom," Arce Teceros said. For example, after a year of the pandemic, journalists at *Alharaca* were burned out, so the site took a three-week hiatus to allow employees to recuperate. They programmed some posts for social media during the break, but otherwise they stopped working. "It comes from a feminist vision," Aguirre said.

> When we talk about changing the work culture, about self-care, we see that in El Salvador, with the situation as it is now, the anxiety and stress of people—journalists—is very great. So we try to be consistent with how internally and professionally we apply this feminist gaze.

These sites recognized the need to support their reporters' mental health, whether by offering assistance applying for grants to cover psychological care, or hiring trained professionals to come to the newsroom. For example, *GK* has a mental health program that partially covers some sessions for workers—something they started around the start of the pandemic, Ponce said. Riera said that when a journalist accused of sexual assault committed suicide, it was especially difficult for her newsroom because one of the site's employees also had suffered sexual abuse.

> At that time, we were all looking out for her because we knew that it was going to worsen the wound. It was painful, but everyone accompanied her ... we were there supporting each other ... What we don't want is for our team to suffer more stress than what we already have to live through in a country that doesn't have water, doesn't have light, is a dictatorship. At least we can try to relieve and have therapy for the people who need it most.

Journalists at these sites also noted that they approach the physical safety of journalists differently than male-dominated news organizations. In Latin America, where most countries have limited press freedom, working as a journalist often comes with harassment, threats, and attacks, both online and offline. Independent journalists, such as those working at these gender-focused sites, are often particularly targeted by governments and their partisan supporters. Waisbord (2020, p. 1031) referred to digital threats and violence as "mob censorship," or "bottom-up, citizen vigilantism aimed at disciplining and silencing journalists," especially those journalists who are woman or racial, ethnic, sexual, or religious minorities. While the harassment may be digital, it often is manifest in physical threats or violence, and results in real-world consequences, such as self-censorship. Knowing this, and that as women they were doubly vulnerable, the journalists I interviewed talked about the importance of understanding how threats and security measures to respond to them needed to consider gender.

Traditional media, "managed by men," treat security the same for everyone, Aguirre said, but it's not the same when a male, female, or trans reporter is sent to cover a story in a gang-controlled neighborhood. "All three face certain dangers, but they're distinct, and the safety measures should be distinct, too," she said. Because *Alharaca* is run by women, Aguirre said, safety protocols were created with women in mind, and they hired a specialist from the Artículo 19 international press freedom organization to train their journalists about the risks of reporting in the streets. Likewise, how *ContraCorriente* responds to harassment is a consequence of having women in charge, Ávila. For example, female reporters are sometimes accompanied while they're reporting, and internal decisions about who covers what are made with understandings about safety in mind.

Feminist media or feminist practices?

Just as many journalists at independent, digital-native news sites are averse to the alternative label, associating it with a lack of professionalism (as discussed in Chapter 5), so, too, have some of these female-led, gender-focused, *cause-based* outlets declined to publicly identify as "feminist" media for its connections to activism. Even for those who claim to be part of a feminist outlet, they recognize the struggle in deciding where to stand in the debate of journalism vs. activism. Still, as interviews revealed, regardless of whether sites outwardly embrace the feminist label, their gender gaze means they view challenging misogynistic mainstream media and practices as their cause—part of their responsibility as journalists. Demanding equal rights isn't activism—it's equality, and that's it, Ponce said. Similarly, Riera said,

> I believe in human rights, and defending human rights and the rights of women and the vulnerable and children, and Indigenous and this issue of different races, is part of the duty of a media outlet. Defending human rights, being a feminist, is not activism.

Rather, it's what journalism should be, she said, adding that all media have a position, and they need to be transparent about it.

The line between journalism and activism is especially fine when it comes to gender-related issues, even though many in mainstream media don't necessarily see it that way, journalists said. As Aguirre noted, for other journalists, gender-related rights remain "debatable," but the responsibility of journalists to defend human rights is "very clear" when it comes to

> writing in favor of people deprived of liberty. It's very clear when you have to denounce injustices to Indigenous groups or Afro-descendants. It's also very clear when an investigation is conducted in cases of defenders of land or the environment. But there is no such clarity when it comes to abortion or topics about women and diverse people. So, I do believe it is an expression of machismo, of misogyny.

That misogyny, sexism, is partly why so many of the journalists I interviewed, while willing to call themselves feminists, were hesitant to merge their feminism with their journalism. *GK* is "of course" a feminist media outlet, Ponce said, but they decided not to use the word on the website because "it generates too much rejection, because it is confused a lot with activism and is seen as somewhat delegitimizing of the rigor of journalism." Instead they talk about having a "gender focus," as the focus on gender and the search for equality are "inherent in what we do." When it comes to militancy, or activism, Mariona noted that *La Nota* is "judged" for being feminist for having a gender and human rights perspective. "Men, heterosexuals and white, also spend their lives doing militant journalism, but no one sees it that way, no one says anything to them because of hegemony," she said. As such, it's important to her that *La Nota's* journalism is credible and professional, so it can be used as a reference, she said. Calling themselves *La Nota* (the story), serves as a tie to professional journalism, so the audience will read them. But the audience also knows they have a position, she said, even though they don't call the outlet "feminist" because of the word's negative connotations. "So, we use 'gender perspective,' or 'human rights,'" she said. Similarly, rather than call itself a feminist medium, *Efecto Cocuyo* describes itself as "gender sensitive," Reyes said, in part because not everyone who works for the outlet identifies as a feminist. As director and co-founder of *ContraCorriente*, Ávila said, she's a feminist. So is her other co-founder, and many of the journalists who work there. But the outlet itself, she said, is a "journalism business" and so shouldn't be trying to supplant feminist organizations to lead the fight for gender equality. As such, she said, *ContraCorriente* is not a feminist news outlet, but a news outlet with feminist practices. Worried about alienating audiences who might balk at the implied militancy in a term like "feminist," these sites thus take feminist stances from behind the protection of professionalism.

In contrast, *Alharaca* opted to use the feminist label, although the choice came with a lot of debate, Aguilar said. "It was a decision that cost us, it wasn't so easy, I think, because maybe we still have reservations about how this will be perceived, because in El Salvador, in Latin America, to call yourself feminist is a little radioactive," she said. As a result, they are careful to emphasize their professional journalistic traits so as not to be dismissed as activists or as mouthpieces. Because most outlets are managed by men, "there's this worry that introducing feminist themes or a feminist perspective means to stop doing journalism and start doing activism," Aguirre said. "It's the insecurity of fragile masculinity ... We cross journalism with activism, but we apply journalistic methods. We're a journalistic medium ... I'm a journalist and we do feminist journalism." The fact that *Alharaca* chose to use the feminist label in El Salvador, one of the countries in the region with the least amount of coverage challenging gender stereotypes (GMMP, 2021b), makes their overt positionality all the more noteworthy.

Even though all these journalists might not have called their outlets feminist media, they all made clear that they took stances, while still distinguishing between the feminism of journalism and that of activists. "We always try to have a feminist perspective for whatever we write," Ávila said. But that's not the same thing as carrying a flag and joining a movement, she said. "I believe we lose a lot if we declare ourselves activists for a single cause, because then we won't have the plurality of voices we need to understand what's going on." That doesn't mean they're not doing activism via journalism, though, she said. "We cover everything that has to do with feminist marches, or reporting on the topic, but we believe our fight is intervening in the media agenda and trying to train journalists, and it's an important fight." In an effort not to "mix" their reporting with activism, journalists at *La Nota* created the Feminist Observatory of Tucumán, a separate entity where they call out media outlets for "stereotypical headlines, or for stigmatizing a victim," Mariona said. They put together press releases with suggestions on how to improve reporting, and send it to the various local media outlets. In this way, they're "training journalists in Tucumán with a gender perspective," Mariona said. "As a media outlet, we can set out a different agenda," but it's a "long process; there are a lot of interests at stake. It's not that they do it because they don't know, but because there are political, economic, and power interests that influence how women and the LGBTQ+ community are represented."

Change agents

These journalists thus see their journalism as a form of activism, contributing to media reform first, with the hopes that societal changes will follow. "When we say there's a need for more women and LGBTQ people to be trained and to be able to make the news and tell the stories and visualize things and have the tools that other privileged people have, I think that's clearly an act of activism, of seeking a certain equality or promoting a certain change in the media," Arce Teceros said. Their actions are making a difference, however small, Mariona said. She recalled a case when a trans woman was killed, and local media outlets reprinted the police report that used masculine pronouns with her female name to refer to her. "We got the main media outlet to change that," she said. A radio station invited them on air to discuss the problem and "at first they tried to justify what they had done, but then they gave us space to talk and we told about the reality of the trans community in Tucumán." Another time, they sent something to the state's largest—hegemonic—newspaper pointing out the problems in an article about femicide. While the newspaper's director didn't respond to them directly, the headline was at least changed, she said.

Efecto Cocuyo also is working to change the industry from the inside, such as with its school for journalists. Beyond training journalists how to use digital tools, it gives them a "general vision" of what journalism could be—*should* be, especially considering that many of the young journalists have grown up in an environment without democracy or independent media. "All of our training is transversal," Reyes said. "It's not that we train on human rights, but that everything we do is intersected by it." For example, if it's a training about how to cover elections, then they talk about gender parity, and the need to focus on the female candidates' politics, independent of gender-related issues. Or about interviewing female experts for stories about the economy, technology, or medicine, and not just using them for gender-specific stories. *GK* similarly offers trainings and workshops, and grants scholarships. Still, Ponce said, despite such efforts, she's not sure *GK* and other similar outlets will foundationally, or structurally, change Ecuador's media system any time soon. Instead, through their content and their training, they're providing an "alternative way to inform yourself," giving readers options to change their information sources until the media system itself changes.

And mainstream media outlets are slowly changing as a result, journalists said: they're using more respectful language, and covering more stories related to gender. "We've seen some changes, or at least they're a little more careful about saying terrible things with respect to femicide or structural violence," Ávila said. Independent, digital-native sites also are changing. She cited a journalism panel she attended that comprised all men, organized by a leading independent, digital-native news site.

> Most of these newsrooms are men, so it's obvious that these workshops, panels, are going to revolve around men ... Now we find out that various of the panelists were accused of sexual harassment. I think all of this has made them see they need to change their paradigms inside the media. And it's not easy, since most of the directors are men.

The fact, though, that these kinds of discussions can happen now shows changes are happening, she said.

Conclusion

As the GMMP (2021b) report showed, having more women in traditional newsrooms hasn't meant more news challenging gender stereotypes. The journalists and media entrepreneurs interviewed for this chapter, though, show that in Latin America, having women with a feminist gaze at the helm indeed can mean changes to the journalism landscape. This chapter found that having a feminist gaze, even if journalists didn't explicitly refer to their sites as "feminist" media, influenced all levels of these digital news sites, from their reason for being to their coverage, gatekeeping and reporting practices, ethics, business models, and work culture. Perhaps most importantly, having a feminist or gender approach also contributed to their perspective of journalism as activism, and their sense of accountability not just for offering an alternative to sexist, hegemonic media but also for challenging and changing mainstream media by training a new generation of journalists with a feminist gaze. In so doing, these sites—launched by women who refused to "keep to their place"—have created alternative, digital spaces, at the intersections of professional journalism and feminism, for citizens seeking gender- and justice-centered narratives to counter the top-down, elite-centered, patriarchal news of traditional media.

5 Generating a Journalism That Reforms, Transforms

In April 2020, shortly after much of the world locked down because of a global pandemic, Peru's independent, digital-native site *OjoPúblico* launched *Chequeos en Lenguas* (Fact-checking in Languages), a multimedia project aimed at combatting COVID-19-related disinformation in six Indigenous languages. In 2021, that project was one of 80 chosen—only 1% of which were from media outlets—to be showcased at the Paris Peace Forum for its contributions to helping solve global problems and achieve a more "just and sustainable" world.

While the fact-checking project—incorporating Google Maps, audio clips in multiple languages, photos, and brightly colored illustrations—is noteworthy for its multimedia prowess alone, what really stands out is the way *Chequeos en Lenguas* embodies *OjoPúblico's* identity as an "innovation laboratory" whose mission is to investigate power, promote democracy, protect human rights, and fight impunity. Founded in 2014 by a group of journalists, the non-profit site's motto is to tell "the stories that others don't want to tell you."

In Latin America, those stories that other media don't want to tell too often are those related to Indigenous communities. Despite the fact that, throughout Latin America, more than 500 Indigenous groups speak more than 400 different languages (Kossman & Walsh, 2020), Indigenous peoples are mostly invisible in mainstream media. The 2021 report from the Global Media Monitoring Project (GMMP, 2021b) found that only 3% of coverage in traditional media included Indigenous people as sources or subjects. "When you turn on the television to watch the news in countries like Peru, for example, you see the television presenters and you wonder what is happening here," said Marco Avilés, a journalist who has written about racism and diversity for *OjoPúblico* (Lubianco, 2021). "Because when you turn off the television and go to the street, Peru is a super diverse, multi-ethnic

DOI: 10.4324/9781003152477-5

country and suddenly you turn on the television to listen to the news and the majority are white people."

Such discrepancies between reality and what appears in mainstream media have long been an impetus for alternative media. Latin America's rich tradition of alternative communication is grounded in a resistance to uneven North-South communication flows (Beltrán, 1980; Dorfman & Mattelart, 1971) and inspired by Freire's (1970) notion of dialogic communication as a way to liberate the oppressed. Its heyday came in the 1970s and 1980s, with examples such as the Bolivian miners' radio, community media, militant radio stations like Radio Venceremos during El Salvador's war, or the revolutionary press in Nicaragua (Barranquero, 2020). Beyond informing the public, these media were aimed at revolutionary changes to inequitable social systems and oligarchic hierarchies, resistance to authoritarian governments, improving literacy and education, and empowering critical consciousness or self-awareness—what Freire termed "conscientization"—in order to build solidarity and foment change (Graziano, 1980; Reyes Matta, 1983).

Underlying alternative media's ability to construct a "new" hegemony (Reyes Matta, 1983) is their opposition to market-oriented, mainstream media: unlike the hegemonic, concentrated, mass media in clientelist relationships with political and economic elites, alternative media have been characterized as horizontal, participatory, and close to the people they serve. Such "popular communication"—of and for the people, particularly the lower and marginalized social classes—recognizes the need to democratize media and guarantee a plurality of voices. Popular, including alternative, media produce counternarratives that challenge dominant perspectives as they seek "emancipation and the improvement in the conditions of life" of marginalized groups (Suzina, 2021, p. 11).

OjoPúblico's Fact-checking in Languages project not only counters dominant narratives by correcting COVID-19 disinformation, but it does so in six Indigenous languages spoken by "vulnerable populations with little or no access to a diversity of communication media" (OjoPúblico, 2020). The fact-checked messages are spread online, via community radio, and through municipal loudspeaker systems—innovative approaches to inclusivity and plurality in marginalized communities. *OjoPúblico's* efforts are worth noting for their bottom-up approach to communication and the way they offer an alternative to mainstream media—key defining characteristics of alternative media. This chapter uses frameworks of ideal-type characteristics of alternative media to explore what "alternative" actually means in Latin America's digital-native mediasphere. Through a textual analysis of the webpages of digital-native sites like *OjoPúblico*, combined with focus group discussions and interviews with journalists from these sites, this chapter shows how these sites' critiques of traditional mainstream media, their commitment to covering and including marginalized communities, their justice-driven approach to stories in the public's interest, and their self-perceptions about identity represent a new journalistic model that moves beyond being alternative or mainstream to create a reformed journalism aimed at transforming society.

Relational, contingent, and fluid

There is no fixed, universal definition of "alternative" media, but by and large, alternative media have been defined in opposition to mainstream media, oligarchic conglomerates, and their exclusion of the public. Fuchs and Sandoval's (2015) ideal-types of mainstream and alternative media contrast actors (producers, consumers, audiences/users) and structures (ownership, control, form, content): capitalist mass media see the media product as a commodity, with ideological content, many consumers, and few producers, while alternative media offer a noncommercial product with critical content and critical consumers, producers, and prosumers. Juxtaposing alternative and mainstream media in this way helps to better explain them (Harcup, 2013), although the risk is that seeing anything outside the mainstream as alternative makes the concept less meaningful (Downing, 2001). Rather than trying to come up with one approach to define the vastness in practices, formats, and content that comprise alternative media, Rodríguez (2017) referred to "media from the margins":

> In the last 20 years, numerous terms have emerged to name media at the margins, including alternative media, community media, citizens' media, grassroots media, autonomous media, indigenous media, pirate media, and social movement media. Accordingly, debates abound around which term is more appropriate and there is an explosion of theoretical arguments for and against each term, attempting to privilege one over the others. I have been an active participant in these debates and yet, today, I've come to think that we should shift gears. Media at the margins exist as a plurality. There are many different margins, and each margin produces its own type of media. (p. 50)

This plurality is in line with the critique of essentialist, binary understandings of mainstream and alternative media (Huesca & Dervin, 1994): most alternative media projects do not live up to the genre's ideal-type (Rauch, 2016), and what is alternative in one context might be mainstream in another (Bailey et al., 2008). Stemming from Martín-Barbero's (1993) concept of "mediations" to explain the multiple, overlapping "interpenetrations" between the popular and mainstream, the idea of hybridity has taken root in alternative media scholarship. Alternative media's funding mechanisms, organizational structure, and even journalists and audiences can come from the mainstream side of the aisle. In recognition of hybridity and the "mainstreaming" of alternative media, Holt et al. (2019) proposed a multidimensional, relational approach that takes into consideration micro-, meso-, and macro-level differences in alternative media, and accounts for differential perspectives from content producers, owners, audiences, and third-parties, like the competition. Context-dependent dimensions of alternativeness, such as when it comes to actors, ownership, financing, production, participation, and traditions, have been identified throughout Latin America (Badenes, 2020; Simpson Grinberg, 1986; Suzina, 2021).

Importantly, the multidimensional and relational nature of alternative media can be extended to digital-native news, especially when it comes to their independence (Ganter & Paulino, 2021). Financial autonomy, lack of ideological affinities to political parties or religion, and counter-hegemonic and anti-media corporation positions are all dimensions of how "independence" has been conceptualized in Latin American scholarship (Carvalho & Bronosky, 2017; Rovai, 2018).

Not all alternative media are necessarily financially independent, which gives independent, digital-native media an advantage, making them closer to the ideal of what journalism *should* be or offer: autonomy for journalists in their writing and reporting, detachment from political parties or ideologies, and freedom from economic and political pressures from sponsors, funders, or advertisers (Carvalho de Magalhães, 2018).

Because these digital-native sites' dimensions make it hard to easily group them with the militant forms of alternative media Latin America was known for in the 1970s-1980s, or the top-down, elite-oriented mainstream media prevalent today, this chapter takes a multidimensional approach to identify their (dis)articulations to the alternative. Suzina (2021) identified three defining characteristics of popular communication in Latin America: (1) bottom-up, participatory, and dialogic; (2) tied to social struggles and social change, and (3) offering an alternative to the mainstream media in order to "occupy the public debate" (p. 8). These features correspond with those Forde (2011) pinpointed in alternative media in the United States, U.K., and

Australia: (1) democratic commitment to encouraging political participation; (2) strong connection to specific communities; (3) inclusion of stories and voices otherwise marginalized; and (4) the critiquing of mainstream media. This chapter's textual analysis of sites' "about us" pages, in cohort with focus group discussions and interviews with journalists, reveals the dimensions of digital-native sites and the ways they meet (or not) the ideal-type characteristics of alternative media.

Critiquing the mainstream

Forde (2011) argued that alternative journalists saw mainstream media as "politically biased, commercially constrained, and encumbered by its principles of professional detachment, neutrality, and the requirement to demonstrate no overt subjective judgment regardless of the issue" (p. 175). Similarly, Suzina (2021) presented popular communication as a way to "occupy" the media by offering an alternative to the mainstream in organizational structure, format, and content.

This ideal-type trait of critiquing mainstream media is evident in the "about us" sections of Latin American independent, digital-native sites' homepages, their crowdfunding campaigns, and their appeals for readers to become "members." Analysis showed these sites see themselves not just as an alternative to the mainstream, but in resistance to it. For example, Brazil's *Voz das Comunidades* said it got its start in 2005, when "traditional media didn't even mention what's good in the *favelas* and the true social problems that residents face on a daily basis."

The sites distinguished themselves by referencing their quality, in-depth, or investigative journalism, and their impact on public discourse—all in juxtaposition to other media outlets in their countries. For example, *La Silla Vacía* said it seeks to offer the "best" independent journalism in Colombia. Its website sets up implicit comparisons between *La Silla Vacía* and other media, with a series of statements starting with "more than": more than making judgments, *La Silla Vacía* wants to provoke questions; more than report isolated events, it wants to make connections; more than belong to power, it wants to reveal how power operates; more than align itself with a political faction, it wants to include the majority of voices. The implication is *La Silla Vacía* is doing "more than" what other news outlets do.

Most of the sites' pages touted their financial independence, specifying their status as non-profits or being transparent about where they get their funding. Such transparency sets these sites apart from traditional outlets, whose owners are tied—often secretively—to financial sectors or political parties. The websites of Mexico's *Animal Político*, El Salvador's *El Faro*, and Ecuador's *GK* are just some of those that provided a snapshot of their diversified revenue streams. For example, on December 6, 2019, *Animal Político* published an end-of-the-year accounting of reader donations and grant funding, specifying: "In no case is there any condition whatsoever to report under any editorial line or on any specific topic. *Animal Político* maintains its editorial independence and decides, without interference, which issues it considers should be investigated." The unspoken was clear: other outlets' agendas are subject to internal and external pressures that affect which stories are—or are not—told.

Focus groups with journalists from digital-native outlets revealed similar critiques of mainstream media's lack of independence. Luís, from El Salvador, noted that one of the problems with mainstream media is their "lack of substance" and the way they "sacrifice their independence and journalism" for economic sustainability. In contrast, he said, his site was "aspiring to quality journalism." Eduardo from Venezuela critiqued the way other media measure success by the number of "clicks," unlike how his outlet considers success to be "influence," and putting important topics on the public agenda.

Bottom-up, community-centric approach

A focus on community, in line with the bottom-up ideal-type of alternative media, also emerged as a common theme on the digital-native sites' webpages, which repeatedly referred to serving the public. For example, Chile's *CIPER* says it offers "journalism in service to society," while Ecuador's *Primicias* offers "innovative journalism committed to society." Similarly, Brazil's *Agência Pública* says its mission is to "foster independent journalism in Latin America" by "combining social concern with independent and credible journalism."

Concern with society's needs is manifest in the topics these sites cover. Many have sections dedicated to topics like gender, the environment, rural development, inequality, and human rights. Such "progressive" topics don't align with the mainstream media's conservative agenda, journalists said in interviews. The website for Ecuador's *La Historia* says its "loyalty" lies with citizens, and Venezuela's *Efecto Cocuyo* says it "gives voice" to "the people" as protagonists. The Peruvian *OjoPúblico* site explains, "In times of crisis—threatened by a pandemic, by news of the impending climate disaster and in the midst of disinformation campaigns—it is impossible to be neutral: we choose the citizen."

Choosing the citizen is key to understanding independent, digital-native news sites as simultaneously yet differentially oriented toward alternative and mainstream media. In focus groups and interviews, journalists advocated for the importance of prioritizing marginalized peoples and their stories. Choosing the citizen, though, means more than just grassroots, bottom-up reporting—it also entails bringing the public into media production processes. One of the primary ways citizens have been incorporated is as paid "members." Rather than erect paywalls in countries with high levels of digital inequalities and thereby further limit access, the sites ask readers to donate in exchange for member benefits, such as access to special content, special events, or the ability to vote on which investigative projects journalists will tackle next (Harlow, 2021a).

In 2015, El Salvador's *El Faro* started its Citizen Excavation membership program, which it refers to on its site as a "community." The term "community" is common across these sites to describe the relationship between themselves and their readers. For example, Colombia's *La Silla Vacía* says it is financed by "a community of users," and Ecuador's *Primicias* says it is looking to "create a community and connect in a constant dialogue with the audience." During focus group discussions, journalists also mentioned the importance of "interacting with the community" and being "close to the community." Also, as Chapter 6 will show, readers of these digital-native sites perceive themselves as part of a community.

Citizen participation

This narrative of building a community of informed and active citizens underlays the participatory discourse on the digital-native outlets' websites, and permeates what journalists said in interviews and focus groups. Many of the sites encourage participation through sections reserved for community contributions. Mexico's *Animal Político* features a section, titled "El Plumaje," with stories from individuals and organizations. For example, the collective VIRAL (Linking Local Action Networks for National Transformation) has its own page on the news site with self-produced articles about everything from preventing drug use among youth to voting initiatives to local theater productions. Other sites, like *Las 2 Orillas* in Colombia, *El Confidencial* in Nicaragua, and *IDL-Reporteros* in Peru, likewise offer versions of "Citizen Story" pages that accept content or ideas submitted by readers. Wanting to be a "platform for dialogue and debate," Guatemala's *Plaza Pública* offers a "How to participate" guide with ways readers can contribute to the news process, such as by submitting opinion pieces, articles, photo galleries, illustrations, or corrections, or sharing information or documents. Importantly, these are not mere letters to the editors—typically the only space open for citizen participation in mainstream media. Rather, these digital-native sites have opened the gates for contributions directly from community members.

At the same time, however, this user content is branded as *amateur* citizen contributions, demarcated from the *professional* content produced by the sites' journalists. This distinction sends an important signal about sites' articulations toward mainstream journalism and the boundaries of professionalism. Facilitating citizen participation in the news process inevitably requires journalists to give up some control, and how much control is ceded depends in part on how journalists perceive their professional roles and identities.

Professional identity

Routines, codes of ethics, and norms (like objectivity) have been used as a way for journalists to claim authority as a profession (Weaver & Wilhoit, 1996). Most Latin American countries, while not legally requiring a degree or license, have established cultural traditions and professional norms defining "journalist," so only those with journalism or communications degrees can get jobs with mainstream journalism outlets. For example, Esteban, part of a Guatemalan association of Indigenous community radio stations, said he is a "communicator," not a "journalist," because he doesn't hold a journalism degree—even though the job he does and the standards to which he adheres are journalistic in nature. Susana, from a mainstream Salvadoran newspaper, made a point to distinguish between her work and contributions from the community. Journalists have "credibility," she said, because they're "professionals."

This drawing of boundaries between amateurs and professionals could be attributed to journalists' educational backgrounds: one survey found more than 93% of journalists working in digital media in Latin America said they were trained as journalists (Mesquita & Fernandes, 2021). Many of the digital-native sites' webpages list their journalists' qualifications, including any journalistic training or certifications they received. For example, on her bio page, the general director of *Efecto Cocuyo* in Venezuela is described as having "developed a career as a journalist from reporting to management to team building." Similarly, the editorial director's bio stated that she "has been part of the most important investigative journalism teams of print media in Venezuela."

Showcasing journalists' credentials not only helps to establish their professionalism in contrast to "citizen journalists" or others disseminating content online, but it also lends professional authority to the sites themselves so they are not dismissed for being small or online-only. Further, the inclusion of journalists' training and experience, especially as related to their time spent working in mainstream media or collaborating with renowned international media outlets on investigative projects, is another way to separate them from the region's amateur alternative media, thus orienting them toward the mainstream.

Focus group discussions revealed the same pattern of defining boundaries as seen on the sites' webpages. For example, Luís from El Salvador said that because social media have allowed anyone to share content, it's important to "distinguish journalism from everything else that's circulating now." Journalists from across the region talked about "leading the debate," "generating debate," and "establishing a conversation," situating themselves as agenda setters and gatekeepers of citizen input. This unwillingness to completely open the gates to audiences is well documented among mainstream journalism in Latin America (Bachmann & Harlow, 2012). Such hesitancy to fully embrace participation is thus a trait carried over from traditional, commercial outlets to digital-native ones, illustrating that while the journalists might have abandoned mainstream media for an independent startup, not all traditional norms and practices were discarded in the transition.

An emphasis on professionalism, then, disarticulates them from alternative media, but also from mainstream media, which they saw as unprofessional for placing commercial interests over journalistic ones. As César Fagoaga from *Factum* in El Salvador said, "If you're acting under an interest that's not to reveal what's hidden and be a watchdog for power, and you're acting in favor of those who sponsor you, that's anything but journalism."

Stance-taking and justice-driven journalism

While the digital-native sites' limited citizen participation in news processes was oriented more toward mainstream, professional journalism, their encouragement of citizens' democratic participation and their stance-taking in favor of certain causes establish an articulation with alternative media. This particular articulation fits with Suzina's (2021) defining characteristic linking popular media with social struggle and change, and Forde's (2011) defining feature of alternative media as committed to democracy and political participation.

When textually analyzing the digital-native sites' websites, the theme of defending human rights emerges as the underlying connection between sites, across countries. For example, Ecuador's *Primicias* says it practices "a journalism committed to defending the rights of civil society." Similarly, Guatemala's *Agencia Ocote* says it defends human rights via ethically reported stories about "inequality, inequity, injustice, violence," to help in the search for "truth" and a "resolution for the problems that affect the Mesoamerican population." The overt defense of anything lies within the alternative journalism field, outside that of mainstream journalism. While neutrality and objectivity long have been hallmarks of traditional journalistic norms—around the world and in Latin America—it's important to point out that throughout the region, mainstream media have *not* always been neutral, but rather supported elite interests, while still claiming to be objective (Mellado et al., 2017). Still, interventionist and critical adversarial journalistic roles, historically common in the region, have waned with the rise of professionalism (Mellado et al., 2012), making the digital-native sites' repudiation of objectivity all the more noteworthy.

Peru's *OjoPúblico* called out the impossibility of objectivity on its website when it took a stance in favor of ordinary citizens over elites. Colombia's *La Silla Vacía* also overtly broke from neutrality: "We do not promise to show all sides so much as to reflect the closest version to the truth because we know that many times one part is more right than another." Such a statement rejecting "both sides-ism" can be seen as a radical departure from traditional journalistic norms, which equate balance in sourcing with fair or equitable treatment of perspectives.

Most sites' missions and values refer in some way to taking a stance in favor of the public's interest. Mexico's *Animal Político's* site says, "We are not alien to the battles of citizenship, nor are we indifferent to the issues that promote inequality and discrimination. We denounce rights violations, we point out opacity and we demand accountability." *Agência Pública* in Brazil says it aims to build gender equality and promote human rights, information access, and democratic debate. Ecuador's *GK* describes itself as doing "in-depth" journalism with a "social impact" in order to "change society, set the media agenda, and make the world a better place. In just one line, shape the future." Even those sites that don't expressly state a stance for human rights or justice still infer it through statements about being accountable to the public, or the importance of journalism for democracy.

As this chapter has shown thus far, these independent, digital-native sites are oriented toward alternative media when it comes to critiques of mainstream media, a bottom-up focus on communities and marginalized voices and stories, and a commitment to social change, all of which align with ideal-types for what popular or alternative communication should look like. Yet, despite these clear alternative orientations, the sites largely eschew the "alternative" label, and deny that they are activists.

Activism vs. journalism that transforms

Interviews with journalists and activists in El Salvador, Guatemala, and Mexico help us to better understand this seeming contradiction. Journalists generally preferred the terms "independent" or "critical" to "alternative." They perceived their stance-taking as done in the name of quality journalism, not activism. These journalists are not alone in their hesitation to take on the alternative moniker: in places like Australia, the United States, and the U.K., most alternative journalists preferred the term "independent," and saw themselves as professional journalists, rather than activists, despite their dedication to social justice (Forde, 2011). While self-identification is important, digital-native sites' rejection of the alternative label should not be seen as automatically disconnecting the sites from the alternative media field, as the ways in which they discussed their independence and positionality suggest articulations with the alternative.

El Salvador

In El Salvador, journalists at independent, digital-native sites rejected the idea that they were alternative, which they associated with activism. Instead, they said, they offered *an* alternative by doing a "different" kind of journalism that was "honest" and "independent." In dozens of interviews between 2011 and 2017 with journalists from multiple digital-native sites, the word "honest" was the most common descriptor for their work. Raúl from *El Faro* said the public often assumes the site is partisan because of the stories they publish and the news they prioritize. That doesn't bother him one way or another, he said, as long as they're doing honest and responsible independent journalism. "We don't keep quiet like the other media do," he said. Julia from *El Faro* likewise said, "We're an honest medium that works to change certain aspects of this country." Another *El Faro* journalist, Paola, said,

> We're different, not just because we're only online, but because of what we prioritize and how we report it: honestly, freely. We've

built a new type of journalism that is founded on the idea of being independent and doing the kind of journalism we want, that the country needs, without responding to the interests of any group.

Journalists' ideas of honesty were interlaced with stance-taking and social change. They saw such interventionism as good journalism, and not as activism, which they saw as being partisan. "What we do is not activism," Luís from *El Faro* said. "If you think we are too emphatic or you think we have certain causes, what I tell you is that we defend them using journalism and for journalism." At *El Faro*, Diego said, there had been an ongoing debate about the site's role in activism. "Journalists should always ... be in favor of social rights, clearly, and civil rights, and human rights, and in favor of vulnerable groups ... but a journalist has to be very critical, also, of the form of activism." Sometimes journalists have to intervene in the public debate and confront power, but that's different than carrying a sign through the street, he said, adding that *El Faro* is "an activist for journalism, for good journalism." Fagoaga said often the jobs of journalists and activists seem alike

> because you see injustices, like for example that there are women enslaved by gang members to care for their children, and you say, '*puta*, this is happening and it's terrible and I have to tell about it because people need to find out about it.' ... What you're doing is defending human rights ... You're not saying, 'I'm going to be an activist.' No, you're doing your job as a journalist but also defending human rights.

Tomás, who has worked at multiple digital-native sites in El Salvador, said he saw defending human rights, freedom of expression, equality, and democracy as journalistic values. "This should be the type of militancy journalists do," he said. Carlos Dada of *El Faro* also said that journalism is not activism, but if they're doing journalism the right way, "with a clear sense of a social mission," then that is how journalism can "transform society."

Guatemala

Journalists at digital-native sites in Guatemala, like those in El Salvador, highlighted honesty and independence as their defining characteristics, preferring not to call themselves "alternative." For example, Pedro, who works in digital radio, said his site is not alternative, but honest, which distinguishes them from other media that do "propaganda, not journalism." Being honest means inclining toward a particular position—"because journalists aren't neutral in the face of reality"—that challenges the status quo idea of what "normal" is, he said.

We have to be clear that a lot of the things we consider normal are not normal. For example, it's not normal for the Indigenous people in Guatemala to live in the most remote lands, the most remote and the poorest. Since the Spanish came to Guatemala, there has been a political-economic process to take away the best lands and that must be understood. And that does not mean ideology, but they are concrete facts. If I consider that normal, that is ideology ... It is a way of seeing the world that is not normal and you as a journalist have to generate awareness that that is not normal.

Being honest also means recognizing that objectivity doesn't exist in journalism, Enrique Naveda from *Plaza Pública* said. "We believe that whoever talks about objectivity is an imposter or ignorant at best. But we do believe in intellectual honesty. We make explicit what our conceptual or theoretical point of view of seeing the world is." Similarly, Jorge, from the now defunct *Nómada*, said,

A journalist has to be professional, but they can't put aside what they think and feel and believe. Media have to take a stance and defend what they believe ... The positions of the media have to be on the side of justice, of human rights, of equality. Because if you're not on this side basically you're on the other. There is no middle ground.

The Guatemalan journalists saw their work as tangential to, yet different from, activism, which they equated with marching in the streets. At *Plaza Pública*, Naveda said, they don't tell readers what to do or which causes to support, but they say "in our judgment, this is a big problem. Others are in charge of designing the solution, not us." While they don't do activism per se, "obviously we say that we are defenders of human rights," Naveda said, but to avoid losing credibility, their opposition and criticisms remain "on the page, not in the street." Quimy de León said *all* media are activists: mainstream media advocate for their economic or political patrons, but no one accuses them of being activists, she said. Her site, *Prensa Comunitaria,* campaigns for children, against corruption, for Indigenous rights, for freedom of expression, and for other "topics we believe society needs to be informed about," she said, calling their work a form of "media activism." Still, they're not out participating in or organizing marches, but bringing attention to causes, and calling on people to participate: "We're not Communists or part of the student movement; we're journalists." And being a journalist, she said, means sometimes "taking a position for one side of the story"—the side that's closest to the reality of Guatemala's people.

Mexico

It's important to recognize that not all digital-native sites in Latin America do the same kind of journalism, or see themselves the same. For example, some Mexican journalists at digital-native sites were more willing than those in El Salvador or Guatemala to call themselves alternative. "We're alternative because our content is independent and because we are trying to see what is happening with victims, with the violation of human rights, with people who have been defrauded," said Felipe from *Animal Político*. Similarly, Andrea from *El Andén* also saw her site as alternative, simply because "we're not the same as mainstream media, right? ... We cover what's happening from another vision." Luis Miguel Albarrán from *Plumas Atómicas* viewed being alternative in terms of financing. "For us, an independent or alternative medium is one that isn't part of a consortium or part of a board of directors that is receiving money. We sustain ourselves with alternative business models, and in this sense, we are alternative," he said.

At the same time, though, other journalists from Mexican digital-native sites insisted they weren't alternative per se, just alternative to the mainstream, which had strayed from journalism's true mission. For example, Daniela Pastrana from *Pie de Página* said her outlet covers a different agenda from a different perspective, and takes a "very political, very clear position" to "strengthen democracy, human rights, and cover the people's agenda." Still, she said, that's not "alternative" journalism, "it's just journalism." Journalism has always had the objective of denouncing corruption and helping people to live better, so that *should* be what media outlets practice—the problem, though, is that they don't, she said. "Just covering elites ... isn't journalism; for me, it's indoctrination, maintaining the system, but it's not journalism."

Like the Salvadoran and Guatemalan journalists, the Mexican journalists also talked about journalism as a type of activism. As Albarrán said, one type of activism is to "go to a march and there's another, which we believe has to do with information diffusion ... I believe our role is within the chain of activism, within the chain that seeks the best information and that seeks the protection of human rights." Rather than side with elites, said Ernesto Ledesma from *Rompeviento TV*, his outlet aligns with marginalized communities and the public generally, which "of course, absolutely, unarguably, categorically, yes, is activism. We don't care if people don't consider us an objective or neutral medium ... What interests us more is credibility ... We consider ourselves an honest medium, professional." The activism they do isn't of the "homeland or death, *compañero!*" variety, he said, but rather requires in-depth investigations, verification, and professionalism to shed light on wrongdoings and provoke change.

Across the three countries, then, the importance these journalists assigned to independence is what held most of them back from embracing the alternative label. They mentioned the public's "radical" or "anarchist" negative perceptions of activists, which they didn't want to be associated with. At the same time, independence did not require objectivity—which journalists saw as disingenuous—but rather it demanded honesty, which meant standing up for the truth and taking a position in favor of justice or human rights. Naveda noted that calling out injustice can result in criticisms leveled against them. "Some call us anti-establishment as an insult," he said.

> I accept anti-establishment as praise. Because the system is rotten, the system excludes the majority of the population ... Now, are we bad for being anti-establishment? No. Does that make us Communists (I say Communists not because I think it is essentially bad, but because that is what they call us)? No. It is impossible to defend that *Plaza Pública* is Communist; it is not. As it is not conservative, or liberal. But we are anti-establishment.

A third-party perspective

While the public generally perceives these independent, digital-native sites as leftist because of their critiques of the status quo—even though most of the journalists deny that the sites have an ideological bent—it's important to consider how other journalists view these sites. The perceptions of their colleagues provide a relational understanding of digital-native sites (Holt et al., 2019).

Their peers from alternative outlets are quick to label the digital-native sites as alternative because of their independent reporting. Esteban, who is part of community radio in Guatemala, said he sees the digital-native sites as more like community than commercial media. "They're doing counterinformation," he said, doing "the work of informing and having truthful information." Providing the truth, without bias toward financial sectors, is enough to make an outlet alternative in Guatemala, he said. Veronica, an activist who works for an alternative publication in Guatemala, included independent, digital-native sites in her definition of "alternative" not only for the way they cover stories ignored by mainstream media but also for their investigative journalism, the historical context they provide, and the diversity of voices interviewed. Mainstream media—which she referred to as "communication businesses" rather than "communication media"—have given alternative media negative connotations they don't deserve, she said. Erik, who works for an online alternative outlet in El Salvador, also said he sees digital-native sites as alternative because of the kind of "truthful" journalism they do, "from the point of view of the citizen." In El Salvador, he said, if you're not part of the mainstream, then people automatically see you as alternative.

Journalists from mainstream outlets also referred to the digital-native sites as "alternative," although they differed on whether this was a good thing. Marvín, a reporter for a major newspaper in El Salvador, said that activist groups and civil society organizations "find more of a voice and a microphone" in the digital sites, which "don't do the traditional journalism that we do in this newspaper. They go deeper into the issues, the information, the statistics … They cover issues without the prejudices with which sometimes they are approached by traditional and conservative newspapers." Miguel, a Guatemalan TV journalist, called the independent, digital-native news sites "alternative" for the way they "cover topics commercial media won't, topics like the contamination of some river by some mining company." They don't have to worry about a conflict of interest with a company that might pull its advertising, he said. He also noted that since the 2015 anti-corruption protests that ousted a president and vice-president, there's been a clear line drawn among journalists: those from digital outlets that support democracy and take a stand against corruption, and other media that don't.

Other mainstream journalists used the term "alternative" pejoratively in reference to the digital-native sites. For example, a mainstream journalist in El Salvador, Pablo, said the problem with digital outlets and alternative media is that sometimes "the journalist starts to define themselves as an activist for human rights," and then they lose their journalistic integrity. Similarly, Yessica, from a major Guatemalan newspaper, dismissed the digital-native sites as "activism."

Conclusion

Mainstream media journalists' categorization of these digital-native sites as alternative could be seen as a way to delegitimize the competition, as journalists from the digital-native sites said. However, the fact that alternative media producers and activists also saw the sites as alternative is telling—not just of these digital-native sites' articulations to the alternative but also of their disarticulation from the mainstream. Despite their professionalism and claim on quality, rigorous, honest, and credible journalism, these sites' orientations toward mainstream media are not enough to fully disarticulate them from alternative journalism. In fact, their orientations to the professional set them apart as *not* mainstream in a media system where to be mainstream means privileging non-journalistic interests, and a lack of independence. As many journalists at the digital-native sites said, they're alternative only in the sense that they offer *an* alternative to traditional media by providing quality, *real* journalism that mainstream media have forsaken.

Hájek and Carpentier (2015), in their study of three self-identified "alternative" magazines in the Czech Republic, were confronted with a similar, yet opposite, situation: journalism organizations that claimed to be alternative, yet in fact exhibited more characteristics of mainstream than alternative media. Rather than dismiss the magazines as being altogether mainstream and not alternative, the authors proposed the idea of "alternative mainstream media," or media outlets that serve as "alternatives *within* the mainstream media" (p. 378). They contended that instead of seeing these outlets as hybrids, we should consider them as falling *between* the "archetypes" of alternative and mainstream media.

In the case of these Latin American digital-native outlets, we see more alignment with alternative criteria than with mainstream, with sites fulfilling popular and alternative communication ideal-type characteristics: critiquing the mainstream and including stories and voices excluded by the mainstream, fostering communication and community participation, and being tied to social change. Building off Hájek and Carpentier (2015), we might question whether we should consider these digital-native sites as *mainstream within the alternative*. However, as this chapter has shown, these digital-native sites' editorial independence is articulated to *professional* journalism—not *mainstream* journalism. Further, their participatory values are linked with alternative journalism, but limited by the boundaries of professional journalism. More than in resistance against a particular political party or system, as is characteristic of the ideal-type of Latin America's alternative media, these sites are in resistance against mainstream journalism and its allegiance to advertising, elite perspectives, and the status quo. Even as they mount their challenge to the mainstream, though, they still rely on the ideals of professional journalism to appeal to readers and validate their existence. Although many are cause-based, they are not openly politically ideological, disarticulating them from many activist and alternative outlets.

Still, despite their professional orientation, these sites' articulations to alternative journalism and activism shouldn't be discounted. Whether on their websites or during focus groups or interviews, journalists from independent, digital-native sites across Latin America exhibited connections to the alternative, fulfilling ideal-type characteristics of popular and alternative communication. Even with these articulations to the alternative, though, these sites reorient themselves toward professional, mainstream journalism by way of denying their alternativeness, and explaining away their media activism as simply a return to good journalism, or as part of their duty as Guardians of journalism. These sites thus occupy a liminal space between mainstream and alternative media, operating from the margins of "professional" journalism in terms of identity, yet creating a bridge to the adjacent spheres of activism, advocacy, and alternative media in terms of roles, norms, and practices. Perhaps, though, as Raúl said, it doesn't matter whether the public, other media outlets, or the sites themselves consider them alternative or not. "What is important is they know we are credible, and we provide something different, more useful, than what other media offer. And that can change journalism."

6 Portrait of an Active (Alternative) Audience

The chapters in this book thus far have built a case for the ways digital-native sites in Latin America are changing the journalism landscape, pioneering innovative ways of thinking about financial and editorial independence, professional identity, advocacy, social media use, and gender. Up to this point, however, most of the evidence has been presented from the journalists' perspectives, or based on content produced by journalists. This chapter considers audience perceptions of digital-native sites, as understanding who is reading these sites helps us better situate the sites' articulations toward professionalism/activism and mainstream/alternative journalism. Ultimately this chapter contends that audiences' news consumption and political behaviors are reflective of how digital-native news organizations see themselves and their remaking of journalism.

With a few notable exceptions, little is known about the audiences of alternative media (Rauch, 2021), and even more remains to be learned about digital-native media audiences. The few studies examining alternative media audiences point to an appreciation for journalists' transparency about their subjectivity (Atton & Hamilton, 2008), and a sense of empowerment (Ewart et al., 2005) engendered by information that helps them make sense of their daily lives (Rauch, 2015). Notably, audiences tend to see their alternative media use as a form of "symbolic resistance" (Rauch, 2015, p. 1007). One commonality among these studies is a dissatisfaction with mainstream media and using alternative media to seek information to help them engage democratically as citizens (Harcup, 2016). This is in line with an earlier comparison of alternative media use among activists in the United States and Latin America, in which Dustin Harp and I found a positive correlation between mistrust in mainstream media and the belief that alternative media should play a role in activism. The Latin American respondents in particular noted the value of digital media for "spreading alternative

DOI: 10.4324/9781003152477-6

information" and getting around the "elite," "biased," and "unreliable" corporate, mainstream media (Harlow & Harp, 2013, p. 41).

Understanding mainstream and alternative media from the audiences' perspective is especially important considering

> members of this audience tend to be written about as being a particularly discerning and socially aware collection of individuals who, when they gather within the conceptual spaces of an alternative or counter-public sphere, have the potential to transcend individual consumerism and become something approaching a public, an active citizenry.
>
> (Harcup, 2016, p. 680)

Downing (2001) suggested that alternative media are inherently linked with social movements, but little research empirically examines this link. The few studies that have been conducted indeed show correlations between alternative media use and political participation, including protest activity (Boyle & Schmierbach, 2009; Chan, 2017; Leung & Lee, 2014). With this in mind, this chapter not only offers a snapshot of the digital-native news sites' audiences but also explores to what extent these readers consider the sites "alternative," facilitating active citizen engagement (Harcup, 2013).

Research conducted about the audiences of digital-native news sites in Latin America suggests readers are elite and unhappy with corporate, mainstream media. My comparison of Guatemalan and Nicaraguan digital-native sites identified audiences as highly educated and politically progressive, interested in financially and editorially independent, credible news (Harlow, 2018). Similarly, another study considering the transnational audiences of digital-native sites in six Latin American countries found readers sought news outside their home countries because the local media were not as independent, objective, or truthful as the digital-native sites (Higgins Joyce & Harlow, 2020). This chapter builds on these previous studies, using a survey[1] of readers of digital-native sites to provide a nuanced understanding of who these audiences are and how and why they use the digital-native sites, thus helping us to better situate the sites' orientations toward professionalism/activism and mainstream/alternative journalism.

Audience characteristics

Survey results showed readers of seven Latin American digital-native sites lived in 19 countries from across the region. Most (69%) were male and were aged 50 or younger (62%). They were highly educated, with most having completed a bachelor's degree (38%), a graduate degree (31%), or at least some graduate schooling (10%). About 42% made less than $10,000 per year, although it's important to acknowledge that the average income per capita for the region is about $8,833 (Statista, 2020). This means that roughly 58% of these sites' readers make more than the region's average annual income, and about 6% make more than $100,000 a year, or more than 10 times the average. Politically speaking, most identified as progressive (32%) or very progressive (35%). The overwhelming majority (94%) lived in urban areas. These demographics suggest these sites are reaching mostly elite readers, and journalists at these sites attribute it in part to being online only. While in focus groups and interviews journalists said they wished they could reach a broader audience, they also talked about the importance of having decision makers as their readers.

Readers of these sites are avid news consumers and social media users. About 93% said they had Internet access at home, and 90% said they go online multiple times per day. Most primarily access the Internet from home (41%) or their phones (29%). Most respondents said they mainly get their news from online, commercial news outlets (35%) or social media (34.6%). About 11% said alternative media is their main news source. About 71% of respondents said they went online for news seven days a week, and 95% use social media every day. About 30% said they access these digital-native news sites at least five days a week.

Their activity online is worth noting for its relation to political participation offline. About 34% said they had participated in a debate or conversation on social media about a topic important to them in the previous year, 23% had participated in online activism, 30% had attended a community meeting about an issue important to them, 35% had signed a petition, 28% had attended a protest, 4% had participated in a boycott, 6% had participated in some other kind of civil disobedience, 38% said they had tried to persuade someone about an issue important to them, 19% had contacted the media about an issue important to them, 16% had contacted a public official about an issue they believed was important, and 39% had commented on a news story on a newspaper's website.

Digital-native sites give readers what mainstream media don't

To better understand the links between digital-native news sites and alternative media, this chapter specifically explored concepts traditionally considered characteristic of alternative media. Overall, the survey showed readers are accessing these digital-native sites for reasons related to both mainstream and alternative journalism characteristics, even though most (88%) said they believed the digital-native news sites were different from traditional commercial media. For example, nearly all (94%) said investigative news was important to them, as was independent/critical news (92%), transparency (92%), objectivity (90%), balance (88%), and credibility (84%)—traits associated with traditional journalism norms and practices. At the same time, readers also valued aspects more oriented toward alternative media: taking a stance against corruption (90%), actively participating in the community (55%), and covering stories and voices normally marginalized by the media (86%).

Readers' beliefs about how the news should be financed also showed simultaneous orientations toward both the mainstream and alternative: about 46% of readers cited advertising, and 40% subscriptions, as how news should be funded. Non-traditional forms, though, also were important: 28% said foundations or NGOs; 22% said subsidies, taxes, or other government funding; and 22% said public donations.

Readers' responses to an open-ended survey question (n = 2,794) about how the digital-native news sites differed from mass, commercial media give us a more nuanced understanding of how audiences perceive not just the digital-native sites but also mainstream media and Latin American journalism generally. Some basic word frequencies offer a starting point. The word "independent" (or its derivatives) was used 133 times in readers' responses. "Truthful" or a variation was used 226 times. "Objective" appeared 221 times, "impartial" 104 times, and "professional" 91 times. "Investigative" appeared 732 times. In contrast, "innovative" was found just 18 times, and "technology" seven times. What these frequencies begin to explain is that audiences value the quality journalism and professionalism of these sites, especially their investigative reporting and "anti-power" perspectives, more than their digital-ness. A thematic analysis of readers' open-ended responses[2] revealed that besides investigative reporting and professionalism, audiences distinguished the digital-native sites from mainstream media according to their alternative agendas, independence, honesty, and objectivity.

Comments from the digital-native sites' readers speak to a frustration with the bias, superficiality, and cronyism of mass, commercial media. Instead of referring to what digital-native sites *are*, readers instead specified what they aren't, contrasting them with mainstream media: they're not "sensational," "manipulated," "biased," "incomplete," "partisan," "servile," "rigged," or "compromised." The sites don't cater to the "interests" of "elites," "corporations," "the dominant class," or "politicians." They don't "fear the truth" and they don't "obey the pressures that affect traditional media." Readers recognized that certain topics, such as those about human rights, environmental rights, women, Indigenous peoples, youth, and poor people, aren't covered in traditional media because they might threaten the "centers of economic and political power," as a female from Guatemala noted. The sites offer "space to address taboo themes; it's refreshing." In fact, readers often used the word "refreshing" or "fresh" to refer to the way the digital-native sites "fill the information gap" left by commercial media, as a male from Nicaragua said.

Unlike mainstream media, respondents said, the digital-native sites provided "professional, investigative, in-depth, quality journalism," as another male from Nicaragua said. Respondents associated concepts like "truthful," "impartial," "objective," "not sensational," "quality," "lack of self-censorship," "balance," "credibility," "ethics," and "diversity of opinions" with what they considered to be professional journalism. Audiences also mentioned how well-educated and trained journalists at the digital-native sites were, calling the journalists "excellent" and their editing and reporting skills "impeccable." A female reader from Guatemala said, "The quality of articles they publish is better than any other media."

Based on the frequency with which the word "investigative" appeared, it's clear that readers valued the in-depth reporting they felt they couldn't get from traditional, commercial media. About 22% of all responses were coded as referencing investigative journalism. The digital-native sites are different because they "specialize in objective and in-depth investigative journalism," one male respondent from Nicaragua said, while a male from El Salvador noted the way the sites are "investigative and without evident editorial limits for economic reasons, like other media." Respondents from across Latin America also referred to the "rigorous," "impartial," "serious," "relevant," and "responsible" investigations the sites conduct. Responses about investigative journalism also were inherently linked to the other themes of professionalism, independence, honesty, and objectivity.

Like investigative reporting, professionalism also went hand-in-hand with independence, objectivity, and truth-telling, as respondents' answers showed they perceived political and economic independence as the foundation upon which honesty, professionalism, and investigative reporting were made possible. A male from Venezuela commented that the sites are "independent, unlike the mouthpieces of the traditional press that, necessarily, correspond to economic interests and, therefore, a political orientation." Similarly, another female reader from Guatemala said the sites aren't "subject to the interests of power or advertising groups," like mainstream media are. Readers said being independent gave the sites freedom to criticize the powers that be, and cover diverse content normally silenced by the mainstream media. "They offer information that other media censor," as a female from Colombia said. Another female reader, from Nicaragua, noted that the sites "speak the truth" and don't hide reality "just to ingratiate" themselves with a particular person or party. They "question the system in every way, with a critical position and from a human rights perspective." A reader who didn't provide their gender or home country noted that the sites are "honest, impartial, without a specific editorial line other than the pure need to tell things as they are, regardless of which political side might be affected."

Readers also associated independence with an alternative editorial agenda, which they said required "bravery." That alternative agenda involved "more reporting in the public interest," as a male Brazilian reader commented, which is "very, very different" from other media. Digital-native sites reported from "different criteria and points of views and ideologies," a male Venezuelan said. The sites have a "different focus," or "unique" focus, many readers said, that is "progressive," with a "human rights perspective," and includes "new narratives" with "different voices" and a focus on "topics important to society." The audience members noted that the sites have a "clear social justice position," and an editorial line with "democratic values." It's "another way of looking at reality" that is more closely aligned with the realities of everyday citizens, and not elites, readers said. They're "committed to society," a female from Guatemala said, and to "telling stories from the people," and not just spokespeople, a male from Venezuela said. The sites present "the voice of the opposition," a male reader who did not give his country said.

Beyond the topics covered, the perspectives presented, and the voices included, part of what sets the digital-native sites' agendas apart in these readers' view is their emphasis on educating the public in order to transform society. More than just "give the news," the sites are oriented toward sharing "useful content" to "make decisions." As a female from Mexico put it, "their purpose is not only to inform, but to enable." The ultimate goal of this agenda is not just to "question power," several readers said, but it's about provoking change. "A clear goal is to contribute to the changes that that our country really needs," a female from El Salvador said. Such an educational emphasis, as perceived by readers, demonstrates an orientation toward the alternative, as alternative journalists have been shown to see one of their primary roles as educating the public in order to activate their political participation (Forde, 2011).

These reader comments show us that digital-native news sites' audiences perceive the digital-native sites as disarticulated from many mainstream media traits, like hegemonic content and commercialism. However, their views of the sites also are simultaneously articulated toward professional, quality journalism. Audiences seemingly want a different type of journalism that they see digital-native sites as the only ones offering: they want a professional journalism adhering to traditional norms about quality, verification, and balance, but with content that follows an alternative agenda that stands up for justice and democracy and elevates ordinary perspectives, thus giving readers the tools they need to participate politically.

Demographics

Considering that until now so little is known about these digital sites' audiences, and knowing that relationships with audiences underlie the potential for these sites' sustainability, it's important to consider not just whether readers think these sites are different than the mainstream, but also what drives them to the sites. The survey data show that demographics matter: age, gender, political ideology, and home country all are correlated with how often readers access the digital-native news sites (Table 6.1). Older, male readers and those who identify as more progressive than conservative were more frequent users of the sites.

Older readers perhaps have more free time since they could be retired or no longer raising children, thus giving them more time to spend reading the news. This tracks with findings from the United States: the American Press Institute (2014) found that older adults keep up with the news more than their younger cohorts. Another study from the United States found most alternative and activist media consumers fell between the ages of 30 and 59, and were male, college-educated, and politically progressive (Rauch, 2021). Still, research generally shows it's the younger audiences, more than older ones, who get their news online. While most of the Latin American sites' surveyed readers were 50 or younger, the fact that age was associated with more frequently accessing the site suggests the sites indeed are attracting younger readers, but perhaps not providing the content they want to keep them coming back frequently. It's worth questioning, then, what

Table 6.1 Factors predicting how often readers accessed the digital-native news sites

	Frequency of access[a]	
	Beta	p value
Gender	−.041	.051
Age	.188	.000***
Education	−.024	.282
Political ideology	.078	.000***
Income	−.034	.137
Live in:[b]		
Mexico	.162	.000***
Guatemala	.040	.095
Honduras	.000	.995
El Salvador	.216	.000***
Nicaragua	.296	.000***
Costa Rica	.012	.565
Panama	.010	.618
Dominican Republic	.012	.550
Colombia	−.016	.451
Ecuador	−.007	.728
Peru	−.003	.884
Bolivia	.000	.988
Chile	−.030	.147
Argentina	.049	.019*
Paraguay	.019	.348
Uruguay	−.020	.319
Brazil	.004	.831
Puerto Rico	.005	.815
Prefer alternative media	.070	.001**
Different than mainstream	.039	.099
Traditional journalistic norms/values	−.042	.098
Alternative funding/products	−.030	.252
Innovative	.087	.001**
Interactivity	.150	.000***
Alternative content	.139	.000***
R^2	.225	
Adjusted R^2	.213***	

Betas are standardized coefficients.
* $p < .05$,
** $p < .01$,
*** $p < .001$.
a [$F(30, 1904) = 18.416$, $p < .001$].
b Living in Venezuela was the reference variable.

more these Latin American sites need to do to reach young people and cultivate a sense of trust that could potentially develop into reader loyalty.

Slightly less than a third of respondents were women, which helps explain the finding that male readers accessed the sites most often. Further, most of the sites studied in this chapter were founded by men. As Chapter 4 pointed out, Latin America's journalism (like that around the world) is plagued by sexism. It's no wonder that content created by men is mostly going to attract men.

Looking at the political ideology of readers, it should come as no surprise that these sites' audiences are mainly leftists. The commercial, mainstream media throughout the region are known for their ties to politically conservative elites, and these digital-native sites make clear that they are different from the mainstream. It follows that these sites' editorial and financial independence would attract readers on the left of the political spectrum who are dissatisfied with mainstream media and its service to political and business elites.

Latin America is not a monolith, despite similarities in culture and political and media systems. Noting the country differences in readership of the digital-native news sites is thus important for contextualizing how news audiences vary throughout the region. This survey showed readers in Mexico, El Salvador, Nicaragua, and Argentina accessed the news sites most frequently. In part, this is attributed to the fact that three of the sites under study were located in Mexico, El Salvador, and Nicaragua. All three of those countries also are beset by high levels of violence, with governments that view journalists as the opposition, often leading to self-censorship among traditional media. Widespread media concentration, commercialism, and clientelism in these countries also help explain readers' discontent with the mainstream media and their turn to the digital-native sites. In Argentina, the media and political landscape is increasingly polarized (Becerra et al., 2012) and fragmented, with the country's "star" journalists fighting to maintain relevance as readers turn away from traditional media, and outlets reduce space for dissonant voices (Baldoni & Schuliaquer, 2020).

Readers who said their principal news source was alternative media also predicted more frequent use of the digital-native sites—a finding that provides further evidence of the sites' orientation toward alternative journalism. Findings suggest readers who preferred alternative media in fact saw these sites as alternative, which is why they accessed them more frequently than readers who preferred news from non-alternative media outlets. Journalists at these sites, who have sustainability in mind, need

98 Portrait of an Active Audience

to consider what about the news they produce is "alternative," and perhaps emphasize these characteristics in order to strengthen the relationships with their most loyal readers.

"Alternative" characteristics

Besides considering readers' demographics and main news sources as potential predictors for accessing the digital-native news sites, I also took into account their preferences for alternative dimensions discussed throughout this book: financial and editorial independence, stance-taking, active media, covering stories of normally marginalized groups/topics, and levels of interactivity and innovativeness.

Regression results showed alternative ways of financing the news (such as via philanthropic organizations instead of advertising, merchandising, and organizing forums and events; $\alpha = .718$) did not significantly predict how often readers accessed the digital-native news sites. However, this is likely a function of readers' income levels: if income is taken out of the model, financing becomes a significant predictor of readership. Likewise, journalistic ideals about what readers want (investigative, independent, transparent, objective, balanced; $\alpha = .842$) did not predict increased frequency of access, and neither did readers' belief that the sites were different than the mainstream. These findings perhaps are explained by the variables themselves, as generally audiences wanted investigative, independent, transparent, objective journalism, and most saw the sites as offering something different from commercial media, thus there was little variability in these reader preferences.

In contrast, what the sites offer in terms of alternative content (the sites' content is more credible and independent than mainstream media, readers can get news not covered by the mainstream, media outlet takes a stance against injustice/corruption, media actively participate; $\alpha = .732$) indeed predicted how frequently readers visited the sites. Similarly, innovative uses of technology, as well as the sites' interactivity (ability to comment and share, facilitating the exchange of ideas with others, interacting with journalists, and making readers feel like part of a community; $\alpha = .782$) also predicted how often readers accessed the sites. In other words, even after controlling for differences in demographics and countries of residence, alternative media content and participatory characteristics still emerged as important factors predicting how often readers accessed the digital-native news sites.

A series of correlations (Table 6.2) further nuance the connections between these sites and alternative media. Survey results show that the

Table 6.2 Correlations of readers' views of the digital-native sites and their preferred media traits

Variables	1	2	3	4	5	6	7	8	9	10	11
1. Access frequency of digital-native sites	—										
2. Different than mainstream	.133***	—									
3. More independent than the mainstream	.203***	.475***	—								
4. Access news not in mainstream	.208***	.480***	.547***	—							
5. Get news about social movements	.183***	.228***	.393***	.417***	—						
6. Feel part of a community	.238***	.238***	.389***	.364***	.433***	—					
7. Stance-taking	.131***	.218***	.329***	.270***	.214***	.218***	—				
8. Active media	.128***	.133***	.217***	.161***	.251***	.336***	.334***	—			
9. Philanthropy instead of ads	.106***	.136***	.181***	.191***	.248***	.327***	.222***	.316***	—		
10. Online/offline protest participation	.002	.040*	.052**	.038*	−.027	.017	.086**	.152***	.068**	—	
11. Prefer alternative media	.019	.039*	.009	.035	−.002	.009	.055**	.048*	.080***	.153***	—

* $p < .05$,
** $p < .01$,
*** $p < .001$.

more readers accessed these digital-native news sites, the more likely they were to prefer alternative media over commercial, mainstream media, and to ascribe to beliefs that media should be editorially and financially independent, cover marginalized groups and stories, be innovative in their storytelling, create a sense of community, actively stand against injustice, and participate in the community and activism—all of which are fundamental tenets of alternative journalism. These readers thus saw these news sites as a form of alternative media, and their motivations for reading these sites were based on that alternativeness.

Mobilizing readers and protest participation

Outside of Latin America, non-profit, digital-native news startups have been found to foster community and democracy (Ferrucci, 2017; Konieczna et al., 2018) by emphasizing the "public interest journalism often missing from regional for-profit publications" (Powers & Yaros, 2012, p. 158). Contributing to a nascent body of scholarship examining how alternative media might mobilize collective action, this chapter also examines protest participation among readers of the Latin American digital-native news sites to consider the sites' role in fostering participation.

Readers' demographics, as well as their media preferences, predicted their protest participation (Table 6.3). Being a man and politically progressive were positive predictors of protest participation. Being from Guatemala positively predicted protest participation, while being from El Salvador, Nicaragua, Costa Rica, Colombia, and Chile were negative predictors. Considering Guatemala has been the site of massive anti-corruption protests since 2015, it's perhaps unsurprising that readers from this country were more likely to have participated in protests. Nicaragua, Colombia, and Chile also have seen massive protests, but while the Guatemalan ones were mostly peaceful and involved broad swaths of society, the Nicaraguan, Colombian, and Chilean protests generally have been brutally repressed by government and police forces, perhaps leading to hesitation on the part of readers to want to engage in protesting. El Salvador and Costa Rica had not experienced the same level of protests during 2016, when the survey was conducted.

Other important positive predictors included alternative media as their preferred news source, as well as a preference for alternative media characteristics, such as media that cover stories ignored by the mainstream, taking a stance against injustice, and media that actively

Table 6.3 Factors predicting digital-native news sites' readers protest participation

	Protest participation[a]	
	Beta	p value
Gender	.046	.028*
Age	−.010	.663
Education	.010	.654
Political ideology	.081	.000***
Income	−.002	.939
Live in:[b]		
Mexico	−.048	.051
Guatemala	.138	.000***
Honduras	.013	.540
El Salvador	−.252	.000***
Nicaragua	−.240	.000***
Costa Rica	−.046	.026*
Panama	−.015	.482
Dominican Republic	−.040	.054
Colombia	−.064	.003**
Ecuador	−.009	.671
Peru	−.006	.763
Bolivia	−.031	.129
Chile	−.047	.024*
Argentina	−.010	.637
Paraguay	−.021	.319
Uruguay	.031	.135
Brazil	−.024	.244
Puerto Rico	−.019	.352
Prefer alternative media	.082	.000***
Different than mainstream	−.017	.473
Interactivity factor	−.062	.022*
Innovative	−.010	.725
Alternative content factor	.169	.000***
Alternative financing	.034	.209
Normative values	−.066	.010*
R^2	.200	
Adjusted R^2	.187***	

Betas are standardized coefficients.
* $p < .001$,
** $p < .001$,
*** $p < .001$.
a [$F(30, 1913) = 15.920$, $p < .001$].
b Living in Venezuela was the reference variable.

participate. A preference for interactivity—another hallmark of alternative, participatory media—also positively predicted protest participation. Notably, a belief that media should be objective or balanced negatively predicted protest participation.

Correlations help provide a closer look at the links between readers of digital-native news sites and their protest participation. How often readers accessed the sites was significantly correlated with offline protest participation. Readers' preference for alternative media over other news sources also was related to online and offline protest participation. In fact, the more readers had engaged in protest, the more likely they were to say the digital-native news sites were different than the mainstream, that they believed media should be financed by philanthropic organizations instead of advertising, that news should be independent, that they read the digital-native sites because they offered news the mainstream media ignored, and that media should take a stance and be active participants in the community/activism. Conversely, it's important to note that a traditionally non-alternative media characteristic—objectivity—was not related to protest participation. In other words, the readers who appreciated the digital-native news sites for their alternativeness were the ones who participated more in protest activities. Such findings indicate that these readers saw these news sites as a form of alternative media, and their motivations for reading these sites were based on their alternative dimensions. This chapter thus suggests that the alternative characteristics that motivated respondents to read these news sites are crucial constitutive elements that link alternative media use and protest participation.

Results also contribute to the debate about clicktivism, or whether online participation is supplanting offline participation (Christensen, 2011). Findings showed that for readers of Latin American digital-native news sites, participation in online activism positively correlates to participation in offline activism. Such a finding is important for showing that online and offline protests go hand in hand.

Conclusion

Despite decades of research on alternative media, we only have snapshots from a few studies—mostly limited to the United States—to help us imagine who the audiences are for alternative news. We also know little about readers of independent digital-native news sites, despite these sites' growing influence. This chapter further focuses the lens to give us an overview of who is reading digital-native news sites in Latin America, and why. The findings herein paint a picture of elite, mostly male, Internet-savvy, educated, heavy news consumers who want independent, quality journalism they feel they can't get from traditional, mainstream media. As noted in Chapter 5, mainstream and alternative journalists viewed the independent, digital-native sites under study as alternative. This current chapter suggests the sites' readers also view them as different from the mainstream, articulated toward the alternative but still oriented toward professional journalistic practices that are mostly missing from the region's traditional, commercial news. Such third-party and audience perceptions of the digital-native sites as "alternative" bolster Holt et al.'s (2019) relational definition of alternative media that prioritizes context so that alternativeness is understood on multiple levels (micro, meso, and macro) from multiple perspectives (producers, audiences, third-parties). The digital-native sites' readers saw value in alternative, non-commercial financing models, and they wanted editorial independence to go along with financial independence. They valued stance-taking more than balance, yet also expected traditional professional norms and practices, like objectivity and investigative reporting. Notably, journalists *and* readers used the same words to describe what they appreciated about the sites. Readers perceived the digital-native sites as offering important features they couldn't get from the mainstream media, like alternative agendas that value the public over elites, independence, and honesty, as well as a concern for human rights and democracy. Whether or not the sites call themselves "alternative," audiences see them that way, and they are reading these sites precisely because they offer an alternative to mainstream news.

Notes

1 In 2016, an online survey was posted to the homepages of seven digital-native news sites (in Mexico, Guatemala, El Salvador, Nicaragua, Venezuela, Peru, and Colombia), and distributed via these outlets' social media channels. These sites were chosen because they were identified by the Knight Center for Journalism in the Americas, SembraMedia, and other such journalistic organizations as emblematic of independent, digital-native news sites in Latin America. A total of 3,871 readers participated in the survey, although not every respondent completed every question.
2 Initial analysis was conducted using QDA Miner to identify clusters of common words across survey respondents' answers.

7 (Dis)Articulations and Disruptions

In the fall of 2021, *El Faro* founder Carlos Dada was in Spain to collect the XIV Antoni Traveria Prize for Freedom of Expression in Iberoamerica, bestowed on the Salvadoran site for its "independent, truthful, and rigorous" journalism. In an interview about the award, Dada highlighted the importance of *El Faro* and other independent, digital-native news sites for serving as watchdogs keeping a check on political and media power. Noting that *El Faro* was the opposite of the traditional media establishment, he explained,

> I think the fundamental difference [with traditional media] is that all the [new] media that have worked are founded by journalists, not businessmen. A generation of new media has emerged with other purposes: to tell things that the traditional media don't tell, to recover genres that were not exploited—such as the chronicle, a very Latin American genre, which we like a lot, and was being left out of newspapers—or the ability to position yourself against power because the priority is not financial results but informational results ... That is the reason why the vast majority of those behind these [new] media decided to leave traditional media, which did not satisfy our sense of journalism as a community service or power watcher.
>
> (Piqué, 2021)

As a news site "committed to human rights," serving as a "reference" for journalism throughout Central America (Piqué, 2021), *El Faro* represents a sort of ideal-type for a new brand of Latin American journalism disrupting how we think about professionalism, financial and editorial independence, innovation and social media, audience relationships, identity, activism, and journalistic values, norms, roles, and responsibilities. The rise of independent, digital-native news sites

DOI: 10.4324/9781003152477-7

(Dis)Articulations and Disruptions 105

throughout the region thus provides the opportunity to examine evolving conceptions of what it means to be *mainstream* or *alternative* in a digital media sphere. By approaching these news sites as occupying liminal positions at the margins of mainstream and alternative journalism, and identifying the circumstances under which they're articulated more to one genre or the other, we can better understand the complicated, overlapping adherence to and rejection of professional journalism and activism. Traditional categorizations of mainstream, alternative, or even hybrid media are insufficient for explaining how these sites see themselves, the roles they have embraced, and the models of practice they have adopted. Rather, we should consider these sites as having challenged both genres, pioneering a new brand that is innovating journalism and its place in society.

This final chapter offers criteria for articulating and disarticulating independent, digital-native sites to and from mainstream and alternative journalism. While these sites have important commonalities that allow us to group them together and categorize the journalism they produce as unique, they are not homogenous. To identify the dimensions of these sites' disruptions to the journalistic field, we must consider their articulations toward mainstream and alternative journalism, as well as toward professional journalism and activism, when it comes to six main criteria: (1) financing; (2) professionalism; (3) audience relationships; (4) news values, practices, and content; (5) norms and ideology; and (6) identities.

Field theory

Field theory (Bourdieu, 1993) offers a useful starting point. Bourdieu (1998) described fields as a "structured social space" where "various actors struggle for the transformation or preservation of the field" (pp. 40–41). Fields are semi-autonomous spheres of action organized and governed according to implicit, accepted rules or "principles of action," resulting in internal homogeneity (Benson, 2006). These shared rules are referred to as *doxa*, or the "system of presuppositions inherent in membership in a field" (Bourdieu, 2005, p. 37) that together create a common understanding of institutional roles, epistemologies, and ethical ideologies (Vos et al., 2012).

The journalistic field, aimed at "impos[ing] the legitimate vision of the social world" (Bourdieu, 2005, p. 40), is structured around two opposing poles: the "pure" representing independence from political and economic interests, and those "dependent" on political and commercial powers. These poles can also be conceived as heteronomous (an emphasis on economic capital) and autonomous (a focus on cultural capital), with professional norms and values mediating between the two. "This model helps account for the ongoing tension between culturally rich, but often economically starved, alternative or literary journalism (*The Nation, Mother Jones*, etc.) and culturally poor but economically rich market journalism (commercial television news)" (Benson, 2006, p. 190). News outlets that claim both economic and cultural capital, like *The New York Times*, are those that wield more power and influence over the rules of the game, or doxa. Bourdieu (2005) lamented that the journalistic field has become increasingly heteronomous and dominated by the commercial pole—a complaint that helps explain the rise in independent, digital-native sites seeking to shift the field back toward the more autonomous pole.

Fields are relational; the journalistic field shapes and is shaped by political, economic, and technological forces. Despite strong stabilizing forces, fields are the site of constant struggle between the "newcomer" and the "dominant agent," battling over "conserving or transforming the structure of relations of forces that is constitutive of the field" (Bourdieu, 2005, p. 30). Whether through normative, deviant, or nondeviant behaviors (Falck & Barnes, 1975), new entrants to the field—such as independent, digital-native sites—can serve as change agents, potentially destabilizing the homogenizing forces as they "pose challenges to the field and ultimately alter its presuppositions and purposes" (Russell, 2007, p. 296). Doxa, thus, can evolve, depending on the actions of the change agents and the reactions they spur. For example, Vos et al. (2012) questioned whether political bloggers, operating from the margins of journalism and thus less "socialized" into the field's doxa, might transform the journalistic field. Their analysis, however, found that bloggers' criticism of news media was rooted in an acceptance of traditional notions of what journalism should be: bloggers criticized journalists for being unprofessional and sensational, and for not being accurate or objective. Such criticisms, the authors concluded, represented the stability of the field, rather than its disruption, as criticisms presupposed adherence to traditional journalistic doxa. In contrast, other scholars suggest that digital technologies, social media especially, might be creating openings for changes in doxa, as the journalistic and activist fields come closer together on Twitter (Barnard, 2016, 2018). Considering these conflicting findings, then, it's important to question: what might disruption of the field entail, especially in terms of norms and practices, organizational structures, and identity? Under what conditions can independent, digital-native sites resist and reform the homogenization and heteronomy of the journalistic field?

Applying field theory to these digital-native sites requires recognizing their "struggle for distinction" (Benson, 2003, p. 122), differentiating them between and across fields (journalistic, activist) and sub-fields (mainstream, alternative). Atton and Hamilton (2008) distinguished alternative and mainstream journalism by considering sub-fields of production: large-scale, mass production concerned with accruing economic capital (indicative of mainstream journalism), and small-scale production, mostly autonomous from market forces and focused on cultural capital (indicative of alternative journalism). However, not all small-scale media inherently seek cultural capital over economic capital, so that within the sub-field exist two poles. At one end is the accumulated symbolic capital, representing prestige, honor, and acclaim, and the other pole is uninterested in or unable to attain such symbolic capital. Professional and amateur production further complicate where alternative journalism fits within the two sub-fields, prompting Atton and Hamilton to suggest alternative journalism occupies a liminal position, at the boundaries of the sub-fields of large-scale and small-scale production, and of activism and journalism. The Latin American independent, digital-native sites under study here similarly occupy liminal positions, placing them at the margins of what traditionally would be considered mainstream or alternative journalism.

Articulation

As Atton and Hamilton (2008) pointed out, Bourdieu's field theory implies the possibility of liminal positions, but doesn't say much about them. Articulation theory (Hall, 1986; Laclau & Mouffe, 1985), though, provides a useful heuristic for situating independent, digital-native news sites in these liminal spaces and identifying what their disruptions of the field(s) look like. Articulation can illuminate the fusion and fissures between the journalism of independent, digital-native sites and mainstream and alternative journalism. A theory and a methodology, articulation assumes meaning is made through contextually specific linkages—meaning (like fields) is relational. Articulation is "both a way of understanding how ideological elements come, under certain conditions, to cohere together within a discourse, and a way of asking how they do or do not become articulated, at specific conjunctures, to certain political subjects" (Hall, 1986, p. 53). It allows for contingent but not necessary relationships between processes, practices, actors, and ideologies, empowering people to "begin to make some sense or intelligibility of their historical situation" (Hall,

1986, p. 53). With articulation, then, we can conceptualize how and under what circumstances discourses are constructed and deconstructed about journalism—digital, mainstream, or alternative—and activism and their place in society.

By considering *context, actors, content, contingency* (when connections can be made), and *constraints* (cultural, economic, and sociopolitical forces) (Weinstein, n.d.), articulation offers a framework for revealing the complexity and constructedness of the journalistic field and its connections, disconnections, and re-connections with other fields and among sub-fields.

Latin America's media parallelism and an elite-captured media system coupled with limited press freedom in most countries created the *context* necessary to push traditional, mainstream journalists to the online realm where they could pursue independence and their idealized vision of journalism. That same context, where mainstream media were seen as advocating for the status quo and elite interests and alternative media as advocating for radical change, positioned these new digital-native sites at the margins of each, allowing them to shape new identities, practices, and doxa disarticulated from the mainstream and alternative. As new *actors* in the journalistic field, the sites have been able to serve as change agents, pushing for the un-learning of traditional norms and practices that work in favor of the status quo and against a community-centric, human-rights-oriented approach to journalism. Their *content* offers counternarratives, prioritizing voices and stories often sidelined by mainstream media, and denouncing the status quo in terms of economic (in)justice, racism, sexism, migration, human rights, peace and disarmament, and social capital. These sites' articulation toward and away from mainstream and alternative journalism, however, is *contingent*. They're connected to mainstream journalism through their elevation of the professional and their gatekeeping roles, yet disconnected by their stance-taking, sourcing practices, and financial and editorial independence. At the same time, their connections to the alternative and activist fields are contingent on their professionalism: their advocacy or "activism" occurs via quality journalism, not via protesting in the streets. Understanding the journalism of these independent, digital-native sites is *constrained* by traditional conceptions of journalism and activism, as well as mainstream and alternative. These sites' mission to offer a different brand of journalism is constrained by the political, economic, and social realities of a concentrated media system dominated by a few companies that have captured most of the commercial advertising market. Their digital-ness, which is what allows them to challenge traditional mainstream journalism, is also limiting, as being online only has created a mostly elite, urban audience, potentially exacerbating digital inequalities in a region where about 32% of the population overall lacks access, and where in rural areas—already mostly ignored by traditional, corporate media—only about 37% of the population is connected (IADB, 2020). The sites' independence in politically polarized countries also opens them to economic, physical, and digital attacks. That same independence, and willingness to call out injustices, also prompt allegations of bias and activism, leading many of the sites to work to disarticulate themselves from alternative or activist media.

This interplay of context, actors, content, contingencies, and constraints thus offers a useful heuristic for helping explain how these sites are differentially articulated toward the mainstream and alternative when it comes to (1) financing; (2) professionalism; (3) audience relationships; (4) news values, practices, and content; (5) norms and ideology; and (6) identities, placing them in liminal positions between journalism and activism, and mainstream and alternative media. Approaching these sites as simultaneously articulated and disarticulated toward traditional mainstream *and* alternative journalism is important for situating the independent, digital-native sites in a new subfield operating according to different doxa in order to build a new brand of independent journalism that is disrupting, challenging, and reforming the journalistic field even as it disrupts the political, social, and economic status quo. Below, each of the six criteria for identifying the sites' differential articulations is addressed to help better illustrate their liminal positions.

Financing

Corporate, mainstream journalism typically occupies the large-scale, mass production sub-field concerned with accruing economic capital, and tends to fall toward the symbolic capital pole, while alternative journalism fits more often than not within the small-scale sub-field focused on seeking cultural over economic capital, but often lacking the symbolic capital (Atton & Hamilton, 2008). Where, then, should we position Latin America's financially independent, digital-native news sites? As we saw in Chapter 2, these sites are mostly non-profit or non-market oriented, prioritizing what they see as quality journalism over profit. Their lack of business plans at the time they were started, a dependence on foundation and grant funding, and no or limited commercial and/or government advertising all contribute to these sites' challenges with sustainability and scalability. That financial independence, though, gives them the freedom to pursue stories and include voices and perspectives normally marginalized by the mainstream, thus bringing these sites critical acclaim for their investigative expertise, independence, and dedication to press freedom, allowing them to lay claim to professional, "real" journalism. When it comes to funding, then, these sites fit more in the small-scale sub-field aimed at accumulating cultural capital. At the same time, though, these sites want economic capital, as they recognize the need to develop a sustainable business model in order to continue the kind of journalism they would be prevented from doing in traditional, corporate media. Further, by virtue of being digital, giving them the ability to reach transnational audiences, and by using social media to reach "new" audiences neglected by traditional media, these sites' small-scaleness is called into question. True, their staffs and even audiences are small compared with most newspapers and TV stations, but their reach and influence go beyond that of a typical alternative publication. Also, unlike alternative media, often marginalized for being amateur, partisan, or militant, these sites are winning international prizes and being hailed for their independence and innovativeness—they're accumulating the symbolic capital, prestige, and recognition not typically associated with small-scale, alternative journalism. In this way, these sites are located at the margins of the large- and small-scale subfields, their financial and editorial independence articulating them more toward the small-scale (alternative media) in terms of economic and cultural capital, but their influence articulating them more toward the large-scale (mainstream media) in terms of symbolic capital and impact.

Professionalism

Professional journalism conducted by professionally trained and educated journalists typically has been the purview of corporate, mainstream media. After all, as noted in Chapter 5, community and alternative journalists often consider themselves "communicators," rather than journalists, because of where they work or their lack of formal journalism education. Journalists at the independent, digital-native sites identified as professional journalists, often touting their experience in mainstream media prior to working at the digital-native sites as evidence of their professionalism. However, it was their recognition of mainstream media's shortcomings, and their decision to go digital so they could do "better," more independent, credible, "honest" journalism, that for them was most indicative of their professionalism. These journalists didn't necessarily consider the work of many of their mainstream colleagues to be professional, let alone *journalism*. As some journalists said, it was "propaganda," or something else entirely, but not journalism. This disarticulation away from the mainstream thus situates these sites at the limits of the journalistic field, which they saw as not truly being journalistic in nature. At the same time, their adherence to professional standards and a professional identity disarticulates them from the ideal-type of alternative media. By occupying a liminal position at the boundaries of mainstream and alternative journalism, these journalists are better able to critique (fairly or not) the lack of professionalism of both, thus allowing them to use their professional identity as a distinguishing characteristic of what it means to work for an independent, digital-native site in Latin America.

News values, practices, and content

The news content produced by the digital-native sites reflects values, practices, and counternarratives articulated more toward the alternative than mainstream. Their editorial independence places them at the margins of the journalistic and alternative fields. On the one hand, it distinguishes them from the traditional, mainstream content that primarily serves the interests of political and economic elites. On the other, it also separates them from alternative or activist media that openly advocate. The sites prioritized a different set of news values from traditional media, finding newsworthiness in citizen- and democracy-related stories. Their practices reflected a justice-driven approach to reporting—exposing, denouncing, and calling for change—that prioritized the public interest. They "chose" the citizen, which meant a bottom-up, community-centric perspective. In line with ideal-type characteristics of alternative media, these sites critiqued traditional, mainstream media; offered counternarratives; incorporated the voices and stories of Indigenous peoples, women, and LGBTQ-plus communities; and fostered community interaction and participation.

Their social media content especially resists a central placement within the traditional journalistic field, reflecting the innovation, creativity, and aesthetic characteristics of the heterodox-creative logics of alternative media (Mowbray, 2015). Suggesting a heterodox-creative logic of digital-native media, these sites deployed social media, and Instagram in particular, as a tool for disrupting traditional, hegemonic, normalized journalistic practices. Social media offered a space for innovating not just in terms of content and storytelling techniques using emojis and visuals, but also in terms of how they responded to digital violence, physical security, and mental health. Such innovative uses were disarticulations away from traditional media's normalized approach to social media, situating the digital native sites closer to the margins of alternative than mainstream media.

Audiences

How the digital-native sites perceive audiences is particularly illustrative of their liminal position between journalist and activist, and mainstream and alternative, fields. Their discourse about audiences suggests a disarticulation from the mainstream: more than quantity of clicks, they're interested in quality of interactions. Journalists talked about seeking input from readers that goes beyond the social media engagement metrics of mainstream journalism. Partly due to the recognition that being online-only is inherently limiting in countries with deep digital divides, the sites regularly offered offline events—some of these events spotlighted the journalists and their investigations, some were interviews with newsmakers, some were opportunities for journalists to learn from civil society organizations, and others just aimed at getting to know readers, their interests, and concerns. The digital sites even turned to analog alternative and popular communication techniques for spreading the news, like flyers, posters, and loud speakers. The goal was to build community and facilitate citizen participation in news production processes, as well as in social and political processes—such participatory values represent a clear articulation toward the alternative.

At the same time, though, gatekeeping remained in effect. The sites created space for citizen content, but audience contributions, while desired, were distinguished as amateur, so as not to be confused with the professional journalistic content. Discourse, then, was articulated more toward the alternative, but in practice, audience participation followed a more mainstream way of viewing the journalist-reader relationship. I would caution, though, that the difference between what journalists said they valued and what they did in practice is not necessarily contradictory, nor a discrepancy illustrating a gap between perceptions and behaviors. Rather, this demonstrates journalists' understandings about the restricted audience participation at traditional, mainstream media—their perceptions of the participatory openings they offer are in comparison with what mainstream media *don't* offer, instead of thinking about how much more they could do to open the gates. This also points to the simultaneous articulations and disarticulations with mainstream and alternative journalism.

From their readers' perspective, the digital-native sites did not fit within the category of traditional, mainstream media. Audiences described the sites as independent, with alternative agendas. The sites' content—with counternarratives, different voices, and a focus on the public interest—was seen as more akin to alternative journalism, as was their in-depth, contextualized, educational reporting. Readers came to the sites for the alternative-minded content, and those readers who preferred their media to take a stance against injustice and to participate in the community visited the sites more frequently. Frequency of site use, as well as preference for news with alternative characteristics, also was associated with readers' protest participation. Even as audiences commended the sites for such ideal-type alternative characteristics, however, they also ascribed value to the sites for certain traditional ideal-type journalistic norms and values they saw as missing from corporate media: professionalism, investigative journalism, truthfulness, accuracy, impartiality, and pluralism. In this way, then, readers themselves located the sites in liminal positions, perceiving them as neither mainstream nor alternative.

Norms and ideology

Recent research points to an increased importance of objectivity and neutrality in reporting that has risen alongside the growth in professionalization in Latin America (Mellado et al., 2017). For most of the independent, digital-native sites, though, this traditional journalistic norm was absent from their missions, as journalists espoused a new kind of citizen-centric interventionist role. Journalists at these sites dismissed the possibility of neutrality, and called out traditional, mainstream media for their false claims of objectivity. All journalists make decisions in their reporting that amount to a type of advocacy, they said, but refusing to recognize those choices and claiming those choices as objective is part of the problem with traditional, mainstream media. Journalists criticized objectivity as one-dimensional, assuming one standard of reality and ignoring the importance of a plurality of voices and perspectives. Their impressions of mainstream media are backed up by research that shows even as Latin American journalists value objectivity, their reporting practices reveal a lack of balance and pluralism (Mellado et al., 2018). Rejecting false balance, the sites embraced a type of interventionism or positionality, where they declared their stances in favor of human rights, justice, democracy, equality, and freedom of information and expression. This took the form of promoting gender and environmental rights, or denouncing discrimination, economic injustice, corruption, and impunity. Journalists talked about their roles as change agents shaping the news media agenda, being accountable to citizens, and making a "social impact." To them, this didn't signify activism, but rather was the foundation of what journalism should be. They had a mission to inform the public, but also to overcome the deficiencies of traditional media, and to help explain—even solve—collective problems.

Their interventionist role in change was particularly evident when it came to those cause-based sites with a gender focus that made clear their gender-equity, anti-hegemonic stances through their content, reporting, business models, hiring practices, and their training of a new generation of journalists with a feminist gaze. These caused-based sites, despite their articulation toward the alternative, are positioned at the edges of journalistic, alternative media, and activist fields because of their resolute commitment to professional journalism—fact checking, honesty, accuracy, credibility, transparency—just not the journalism of traditional, corporate media. Not all independent, digital-native sites are explicitly cause-based, however. While some, like *Alharaca*, identify as overtly feminist media, others, like *La Nota,* express a gender or human rights "perspective." *El Faro,* for example, is not caused-based, but still takes a stand against corruption and for human rights, using the hashtag #PeriodismoIncómodo (uncomfortable journalism) and on its website proclaiming a journalism that "does not keep quiet when the powerful lie." It is dedicated to independent, investigative journalism that "is a way to transform society." These sites' stance-taking and change-agent roles distinguish them from the purported objectivity of traditional journalism. Yet, their stance-taking also is a way they lay claim to quality journalism—*real* journalism doesn't necessarily require the sites to be cause-based, but it does require the defense of human rights, the public interest, and democracy, and thus is not always compatible with neutrality. The positionality of these sites, caused-based or not, orients them toward the alternative, while their rejection of the traditional understanding of objectivity disarticulates from the mainstream. These sites are not necessarily ideological in the sense of the political projects of alternative media, but, unlike traditional, mainstream media, they are driven by ideals related to justice, human rights, democracy, and independence. Such a brand of journalism thus occupies a liminal position at the boundaries of mainstream and alternative journalism, and professionalism and activism.

Identity

Most of the digital-native sites, even the cause-based ones, did not overtly identify as "alternative." In interviews, journalists from these sites thought of themselves as professional journalists, not activists. However, neither did they identify as being part of traditional, mainstream media. The conventional conceptions of mainstream and alternative journalism don't align with how they see themselves or the roles and responsibilities they embrace. From the margins of the mainstream and alternative media fields, and activism and professional journalism fields, they've positioned themselves within a new journalistic Guardian identity (Harlow & Chadha, 2019) that is human-centered, anti-sexist, and pro-democracy, -equity, and -justice. It's grounded in a commitment to the public interest and the centering of citizens as the protagonists. In this way, they see themselves as producing a better type of journalism. They extol an identity of independence, concerned with protecting quality journalism, highlighting their editorial and financial autonomy as what disarticulates them from mainstream *and* alternative media. That independence requires a certain criticality toward the status quo, though, setting them up as oppositional, and leading to them being framed as activists, or as alternative media producers, often as a way to delegitimize them and dismiss any challenge they present to political, economic, or media powers. Such oppositional framing, however, emboldens their claims to independence, further strengthening their identity as disarticulated from mainstream and alternative journalism.

Disruptions

Independent, digital-native news sites in Latin America are thus changing—breaking down and rebuilding—doxa from a liminal position. As they work to reshape—*ameliorate*—the journalistic field, they're carving out a new subfield, building new forms of cultural and economic capital, allowing them to have more say over accepted norms and practices within the journalistic field. Changes to the journalistic field are slow and unlikely, activated by a shock or crisis—like those brought on by technological changes and their resulting impact on the news industry, such as in terms of revenues, audience trust, and fragmentation. While 15 years ago Benson (2006) doubted that the Internet at the time had imposed such a shock on the news media system—"Who are the vaunted bloggers and small media supposedly transforming the media sphere?" (p. 193)—we can now see that the possibilities of the digital sphere and dissatisfaction with traditional media have created the shock necessary to disrupt the system and foment a different brand of journalism in Latin America that is in resistance to traditional, market-oriented, mainstream media and its allegiance to political and economic elites. Serving as change agents, these sites are ameliorating traditional, mainstream journalism in terms of expectations about who funds the news, whom journalism serves, and what responsibility journalism has to take a stance for justice and the public interest. At the same time that they're disrupting traditional doxa and established ways of doing journalism, they're also reinvigorating others they view as having been sidelined or altogether discarded by most traditional, corporate media: independence, investigative journalism, watchdog journalism, rigor, truth, accountability, and professionalism.

Examining independent, digital-native sites from macro-, meso-, and micro levels helps to further show where these sites are disrupting the journalistic field. At the macro-level, these independent, digital-native sites play a different role than mainstream media. These sites' discourse emphasizes an ideal-type of professional journalism that can transform society, putting citizens' interests and the public good above economic or political benefits. At the meso-, or organizational, level, the sites are simultaneously articulated toward and against the mainstream. Their news production processes are oriented toward traditional conceptions of journalism such as when it comes to gatekeeping, the separation between professional and amateur content, or accuracy and fact-checking. Their business models and sourcing practices, however, go against the mainstream, as do their news values and practices founded on financial and editorial independence. Lastly, at the micro-level, the journalists producing the news are professionally trained, and embrace a professional identity, articulating them toward professional, mainstream journalism, even as that identity also explicitly separates them from the mainstream. Further, the content they produce offers an alternative to the mainstream, and provides counternarratives that challenge the status quo.

In these ways, then, independent, digital-native news sites have moved beyond conventional notions of alternative, mainstream, or hybrid media. They've constructed a more professional, idealized journalistic model of practice than that of traditional mainstream or alternative journalism. Such categories don't adequately explain what they do or how they see themselves. These sites' human rights-centered, justice-driven journalism—articulated more to the alternative in terms of values but toward the mainstream in terms of professionalism—is not unique to Latin America, but can serve as a model going forward elsewhere. Around the globe, with political polarization and social unrest reaching new highs and trust in news media plummeting, there's urgency for a different type of journalism that stands up in the face of injustice, and is committed to bringing in a diversity of opinions and voices by serving those groups traditionally marginalized by power hierarchies. For example, we see this movement in the United States, as some journalists distance themselves from false balance and traditional notions of objectivity, and articulate themselves toward more inclusive, empathetic reporting and stance-taking in favor of racial justice (Valentine et al., 2021). In July 2021, NPR updated its ethics policy to allow journalists to protest and "express support for democratic, civic values that are core to NPR's work, such as, but not limited to: the freedom and dignity of human beings, the rights of a free and independent press, the right to thrive in society without facing discrimination on the basis of race, ethnicity, gender, sexual identity, disability, or religion" (McBride, 2021). Compared with the Latin American sites, though, NPR is late to recognize that quality, professional journalism and stance-taking for human rights are not only *not* mutually exclusive, but that one *demands* the other. These Latin American sites have developed a distinct identity and understanding of journalism—its purpose and practice—that help us overcome the (Global North's) limited view of public vs. private media, or alternative vs. mainstream journalism.

Ameliorating the mainstream

Throughout this book, I've shown how independent, digital-native news sites in Latin America are disrupting the journalistic field. Rather than representing a merging of alternative and mainstream, or professional journalism and between activism fields, these sites have innovated a new brand of journalism. Importantly, that brand of journalism is made possible by their very digital-ness: their disarticulations from the mainstream, such as in terms of financing and content, wouldn't have been as likely with the economic ties that come with paying for the pricey infrastructure of a print or broadcast outlet. Going digital gave them the independence needed to innovate a different way of doing journalism. Their journalism, through its articulations with and disarticulations from traditional, mainstream media, serves to contest accepted journalistic norms, values, and practices. Herein I've identified funding; professionalism; audience relationships; news values, practices, and content; norms and ideology; and identities as six main ways these sites have changed the journalism landscape. Going forward, these six elements can serve as criteria to evaluate news outlets' articulations toward and away from mainstream and alternative journalism to understand the extent to which they are challenging journalistic doxa, serving as change agents ameliorating the journalistic field as they move toward a new journalistic identity with a different purpose and different practices.

Not all independent, digital-native sites will exhibit the same strength of (dis)articulations across the six criteria. These sites are not a monolith: sites that are explicitly cause-based might show a stronger articulation toward the alternative in terms of norms and ideology or identity than the more general news or investigative sites. Country also can make a difference, as lower levels of press freedom or media systems with stronger clientelist ties could prompt more of a disarticulation from corporate, mainstream media but more of an articulation toward an idealized professional journalism. What these criteria allow us to pinpoint, then, are the ways in which independent, digital-native sites can disrupt the traditional journalistic field.

The growth of independent, digital-native news sites in Latin America and around the globe, and their liminal position between journalism and activism, and the mainstream and alternative, create an opportunity to rethink how—and why—we classify news outlets. In an ever-more diverse, fragmented, and constantly evolving media sphere, journalism researchers must be nimbler in how they categorize journalisms, especially when it comes to the application of normative and professional standards in a field undergoing a transformation in doxa. Developing criteria to assess outlets' articulations is a first step toward identifying the place—and catalytic influence—of independent, digital-native sites in a changing media landscape. The six criteria this book has focused on are just a starting point. These sites' orientations toward and away from mainstream and alternative journalism are not an attempt merely to overcome any deficiencies of, or fill any gaps left by, one or the other. Rather, they have re-imagined a sui generis brand of journalism with a distinct identity that challenges and disrupts the journalistic, activist, mainstream, and alternative fields, offering the possibility of an innovative approach to journalism that advocates for professional and rigorous yet human rights-centric, justice-driven reporting. There remains much to be learned about how the rise of independent, digital-native sites around the world will change the production and reception of different types of journalism, and what that will mean in the face of increasing polarization, partisan media, attacks on journalists, and threats to democracy. Still, as we have seen throughout this book, these Latin American sites are providing answers to the existential questions about journalism, activism, professionalism, and advocacy that for too long have gone unanswered or been silenced by traditional norms and practices. By centering new values, reclaiming abandoned ones, and critiquing traditional, corporate, mainstream media, these sites are redefining not just good journalism, but *real* journalism, offering best practices and valuable lessons to be learned for digital news projects worldwide.

A lighthouse

On *El Faro's* 20th anniversary, in 2018, *The New York Times* profiled the Salvadoran news site as a beacon for Latin American journalism, highlighting its international prestige and its prioritization of "lines of action" in coming years, including "gender justice, investigation of the privileged, horizontal and respectful dialogue between writers and readers, [and] inspired mentorship" (Carrión, 2018). Just three years later, though, at the close of 2021's Central American Forum that *El Faro* hosted in person after a virtual hiatus for the pandemic in 2020, optimism about *El Faro* and journalism's potential for change was waning. As journalist Carlos Martínez wrote in a column the site published in November 2021,

> We have told ourselves ... that if we did our job well, that if we could be in-depth to explain our societies, if we verified and double-verified, if we chased the money trail, if we controlled the exercise of power, if we always doubted the official version, if we gave voice to the voiceless, if we became rabid dogs in search of the truth, even if we never reached it ... our countries, our citizenships—the men and women that compose it—would be freer, stronger and less at the mercy of pied pipers peddling miraculous smoke. It has not been so.

In a region beset by organized crime, government corruption, aborted justice, and attacks on freedom of expression, the journalism of independent news sites like *El Faro* becomes all the more challenging, exacting, and essential. As Martínez wrote,

Perhaps, I think, the journey that we undertook when we decided to dedicate ourselves to our profession as journalists is one without a destination, that ours is not to arrive, but to be on the stairs. That we do not change the world, and that learning it is the only possible goal. Perhaps what remains is to cling to convictions and attend to the hurricanes believing, hoping, that it is true that breaking the silence, that lighting up the shadows, saves someone from something.

References

Alvarado Mejias, D., Grillet, R., Chirinos, M., Contreras, Y., & Agelvis, C. (2019). 881: la lista de la censura digital en Venezuela. IPYS. Available at https://ipysvenezuela.org/alerta/balance-especial-ipysve-881-la-lista-de-la-censura-digital-en-venezuela/

American Press Institute. (2014). Social and demographic differences in news habits and attitudes. Available at https://www.americanpressinstitute.org/publications/reports/survey-research/social-demographic-differences-news-habits-attitudes/

Artz, L. (Ed.). (2017). *The pink tide: Media access and political power in Latin America*. Rowman & Littlefield.

Atton, C. (2003). Ethical issues in alternative journalism. *Ethical Space: The International Journal of Communication Ethics, 1*(1), 26–31.

Atton, C. & Hamilton, J.F. (2008). *Alternative journalism*. Sage.

Atton, C. & Wickenden, E. (2005). Sourcing routines and representation in alternative journalism: A case study approach. *Journalism Studies, 6*(3), 347–359.

Bachmann, I. (2020). Gender and news. In K. Ross, I. Bachmann, V. Cardo, S. Moorti, & M. Scarcelli (Eds.), *The international encyclopedia of gender, media, and communication*. doi:10.1002/9781119429128.iegmc208

Bachmann, I. & Harlow, S. (2012). Opening the gates: Interactive and multimedia elements of newspaper websites in Latin America. *Journalism Practice, 6*(2), 217–232.

Bachmann, I. & Proust, V. (2020). Old concerns, renewed focus and novel problems: Feminist communication theory and the Global South. *Annals of the International Communication Association, 44*(1), 67–80.

Badenes, D. (2020). *Mapas para una historia intelectual de la comunicación popular: Ideas, contextos y prácticas editoriales de los '60 y '70 en América Latina* (Doctoral dissertation, Universidad Nacional de La Plata. Facultad de Humanidades y Ciencias de la Educación).

Bailey, O., Cammaerts, B., & Carpentier, N. (2008). *Understanding alternative media*. Maidenhead: Open University Press/McGraw Hill.

Baldoni, M., & Schuliaquer, I. (2020). Los periodistas estrella y la polarización política en la Argentina. Incertidumbre y virajes fallidos tras las elecciones presidenciales. *Más Poder Local*, (40), 14–16.

Banegas Flores, C. (2016). Bolivia. En: R. Salaverría (coord.). *Ciberperiodismo en Iberoamérica* (pp. 21–35). España: Fundación Telefónica y Editorial Ariel, S.A.

Barnard, S.R. (2016). 'Tweet or be sacked': Twitter and the new elements of journalistic practice. *Journalism*, *17*(2), 190–207.

Barnard, S.R. (2018). Tweeting# Ferguson: Mediatized fields and the new activist journalist. *New Media & Society*, *20*(7), 2252–2271.

Barranquero, A. (2020). De-westernizing alternative media studies: Latin American versus Anglo-Saxon approaches from a comparative communication research perspective. In J. Servaes (Ed.), *Handbook of communication for development and social change* (pp. 329–340). Singapore: Springer. doi:10.1007/978-981-15-2014-3_69

Becerra, M., Marino, S., & Mastrini, G. (2012). *Mapping digital media: Argentina*. New York: Open Society Foundations.

Becerra, M. & Mastrini, G. (2010). Concentración de los medios en América Latina: Tendencias de un nuevo siglo. *Contratexto*, (18), 41–64.

Beers, D. (2006). The public sphere and online, independent journalism. *Canadian Journal of Education/Revue*, *29*(1), 109–130.

Beltrán, S.L.R. (1980). A farewell to Aristotle: 'Horizontal' communication. *Communication*, *5*(1), 5–41.

Bennett, W.L. (2017). Foreword: What is media activism. In *Media activism in the digital age* (pp. xiv–xvi). New York, NY: Routledge.

Bennett, W.L. & Segerberg, A. (2013). *The logic of connective action: Digital media and the personalization of contentious politics*. Cambridge University Press.

Benson, R. (2003). Commercialism and critique: California's alternative weeklies. In J. Curran & N. Couldry (Eds.), *Contesting media power: Alternative media in a networked world*, (pp. 111–127). Rowman and Littlefield Publishers, Inc.

Benson, R. (2006). News media as a "journalistic field": What Bourdieu adds to new institutionalism, and vice versa. *Political Communication*, *23*(2), 187–202.

Berger, J. & Milkman, K.L. (2012). What makes online content viral? *Journal of Marketing Research*, *49*(2), 192–205.

Berry, J.W. & Kalin, R. (1995). Multicultural and ethnic attitudes in Canada: An Overview of the 1991 national survey. *Canadian Journal of Behavioral Science*, *27*, 301–320.

Borges-Rey, E. (2015). News images on Instagram: The paradox of authenticity in hyperreal photo reportage. *Digital Journalism*, *3*(4), 571–593.

Bourdieu, P. (1993). *The field of cultural production. Essays on art and literature*. Cambridge: Polity Press.

Bourdieu, P. (1998). *On television*. New York: The New Free Press.

Bourdieu, P. (2005). The political field, the social science field, and the journalistic field. In R. Benson & E. Neveu (Eds.), *Bourdieu and the journalistic field* (pp. 29–47). Cambridge: Polity Press.

References 123

Boyle, M. & Schmierbach, M. (2009). Media use and protest: The role of mainstream and alternative media use in predicting traditional and protest participation. *Communication Quarterly*, *57*(1), 1–17.

Bright, J. & Nicholls, T. (2014). The life and death of political news: Measuring the impact of the audience agenda using online data. *Social Science Computer Review*, *32*(2), 170–181.

Carrión, J. (2018). El Faro: dos décadas iluminando al periodismo de investigación. *The New York Times*. Available at https://www.nytimes.com/es/2018/06/19/espanol/america-latina/el-faro-periodismo-de-investigacion.html

Carter, C., Steiner, L., & Allan, S. (Eds.). (2019). *Journalism, gender and power*. Routledge.

Carvalho, G. & Bronosky, M. (2017). Jornalismo alternativo no Brazil: do impresso ao digital. *Pauta Geral – Estudos em Jornalismo*, *4*(1), 21–29.

Carvalho de Magalhães, E. (2018). Jornalistas empreendedores: o segmento progressista-como nicho de mercadona web. *Aurora: Revista de Arte, Mídia e Política*, *18*(32), 110–127.

Chan, M. (2017). Media use and the social identity model of collective action: Examining the roles of online alternative news and social media news. *Journalism & Mass Communication Quarterly*, *94*(3), 663–681.

Christensen, C.M. (2003). *The innovator's dilemma: The revolutionary book that will change the way you do business*. New York: Harper Collins.

Christensen, H.S. (2011). Political activities on the Internet: Slacktivism or political participation by other means? *First Monday*, *16*(2). doi: 10.5210/fm.v16i2.3336

Couldry, N. (2007). Part 1: Researching media internationalization: Comparative media research as if we really mean it. *Global Media and Communication*, *3*(3), 247–271.

Crunchbase (2020). *A decade in review: Funding to the female founders*. Available at https://about.crunchbase.com/female-founder-report-2020/

Cueva Chacón, L.M. & Saldaña, M. (2021). Stronger and safer together: Motivations for and challenges of (trans) national collaboration in investigative reporting in Latin America. *Digital Journalism*, *9*(2), 196–214.

Dorfman, A. & Mattelart, A. (1971). How to read Donald Duck: Imperialist ideology in the Disney comic. In A. Gumucio-Dagron & T. Tufte (Eds.), *Communication for Social Change Anthology: Historical and Contemporary Readings* (Vol. 1, pp. 49–54). South Orange, NJ: Communication for Social Change Consortium, Inc.

Downing, J. (2001). *Radical media: Rebellious communication and social movements*. Thousand Oaks: Sage Publications.

Drucker, P. (1985). *Innovation and entrepreneurship*. New York: Harper & Row.

Emerson, R.M., Fretz, R.I., & Shaw, L.L. (1995). *Writing ethnographic fieldnotes*. Chicago: University of Chicago Press.

Enli, G. & Simonsen, C.A. (2018). 'Social media logic' meets professional norms: Twitter hashtags usage by journalists and politicians. *Information, Communication & Society*, *21*(8), 1081–1096.

Estarque, M. (2020). Women lead independent digital media in Latin America, but this isn't the case in traditional media. *LatAm Journalism Review*. Available at https://latamjournalismreview.org/articles/women-lead-independent-digital-media-in-latin-america-but-this-isnt-the-case-in-traditional-media/

Ewart, J., Meadows, M., Forde, S., & Foxwell, K. (2005, November). Though the ears of the audience: Emerging definitions of news from community radio audiences. In *Journalism Education Conference*, Griffith University (Vol. 29).

Falck, H.S. & Barnes, R.E. (1975). The change agent in the organization. *Administration in Mental Health*, 3(1), 3–11.

Fauchart, E. & Gruber, M. (2011). Darwinians, communitarians, and missionaries: The role of founder identity in entrepreneurship. *Academy of Management Journal*, 54(5), 935–957.

Ferrucci, P. (2017). Exploring public service journalism: Digitally native news nonprofits and engagement. *Journalism & Mass Communication Quarterly*, 94(1), 355–370.

Ferrucci, P., & Vos, T. (2017). Who's in, who's out? Constructing the identity of digital journalists. *Digital Journalism*, 5(7), 868–883.

Festa, R. (1986). Movimientos sociales, comunicación popular y alternativa. In R. Festa & C.E. Lins da Silva (Eds.), *Comunicación Popular y Alternativa*. Buenos Aires: Ediciones Paulinas.

Flores-Márquez, D. (2021). Digital media and emancipation in Latin American communication thinking. In *The evolution of popular communication in Latin America* (pp. 191–208). Cham: Palgrave Macmillan.

Foley, D.E. (2002). Critical ethnography: The reflexive turn. *International Journal of Qualitative Studies in Education*, 15(4), 469–490.

Forde, S. (2011). *Challenging the news: The journalism of alternative and community media*. Basingstoke: Palgrave Macmillan.

Freedman, D. (2017). A return to prime-time activism: Social movement theory and the media. In *Media activism in the digital age* (pp. 120–133). Routledge.

Freire, P. (1970). *Pedagogy of the oppressed*. New York: Continuum International Publishing Group.

Fuchs, C. & Sandoval, M. (2015). The political economy of capitalist and alternative social media. In *The Routledge Companion to Alternative and Community Media* (pp. 183–194). Routledge.

Ganter, S.A. & Paulino, F.O. (2021). Between attack and resilience: The ongoing institutionalization of independent digital journalism in brazil. *Digital Journalism*, 9(2), 235–254.

García-Perdomo, V. (2021). How social media influence TV newsrooms online engagement and video distribution. *Journalism & Mass Communication Quarterly*. doi:10.1177/10776990211027864

García-Perdomo, V. & Magaña, M.I. (2020). The adoption of technology and innovation among native online news media in Colombia. *International Journal of Communication*, 14, 20.

References

García-Perdomo, V., Salavarría, R., Kilgo, D.K., & Harlow, S. (2018). To share or not to share: The influence of news values and topics on popular social media content in the United States, Brazil, and Argentina. *Journalism Studies*, *19*(8), 1180–1201.

Geertsema-Sligh, M. (2014). Gender mainstreaming in journalism education. In M. Geertsema-Sligh (Ed.), *Media and gender: A scholarly agenda for the global alliance on media and gender* (pp. 70–73). UNESCO. https://digitalcommons.butler.edu/ccom_papers/74

GMMP (2021a). GMMP results: Glacial progress towards media gender equality 25 years on. *Global Media Monitoring Project*. Available at https://waccglobal.org/gmmp-results-glacial-progress-towards-media-gender-equality-25-years-on/

GMMP (2021b). 6th global media monitoring project show quantitative gains, qualitative losses. *Global Media Monitoring Project*. Available at: https://waccglobal.org/6th-global-media-monitoring-project-show-quantitative-gains-qualitative-losses/

González de Bustamante, C. & Relly, J.E. (2021). *Surviving Mexico: Resistance and resilience among journalists in the twenty-first century*. University of Texas Press.

Graziano, M. (1980). Para una definición alternativa de la comunicación [For an alternative definition of communication]. ININCO, No. 1.

Guerrero, M. & Márquez-Ramírez, M. (Eds.) (2014). *Media systems and communication policies in Latin America*. London, England: Palgrave Macmillan.

Gupta, V.K., Turban, D.B., Wasti, S.A., & Sikdar, A. (2009). The role of gender stereotypes in perceptions of entrepreneurs and intentions to become an entrepreneur. *Entrepreneurship Theory and Practice*, *33*(2), 397–417.

Hågvar, Y.B. (2019). News media's rhetoric on Facebook. *Journalism Practice*, *13*(7), 853–872.

Haim, M., Karlsson, M., Ferrer-Conill, R., Kammer, A., Elgesem, D., & Sjøvaag, H. (2021). You should read this study! It investigates Scandinavian social media logics. *Digital Journalism*, *9*(4), 406–426.

Hájek, R. & Carpentier, N. (2015). Alternative mainstream media in the Czech Republic: beyond the dichotomy of alternative and mainstream media. *Continuum*, *29*(3), 365–382.

Hall, S. (1986). On postmodernism and articulation: An interview with Stuart Hall. In L. Grossberg (Ed.), *Journal of Communication Inquiry*, *10*(2), 45–60.

Hamilton, J.F. (2009). *Democratic communications: Formations, projects, possibilities*. Lexington Books.

Hanitzsch, T., Hanusch, F., Ramaprasad, J., & De Beer, A.S. (Eds.). (2019). *Worlds of journalism: Journalistic cultures around the globe*. Columbia University Press.

Harcup, T. (2013). *Alternative journalism, Alternative voices*. Routledge.

Harcup, T. (2016). Asking the readers: Audience research into alternative journalism. *Journalism Practice*, *10*(6), 680–696.

Harlow, S. (2018). Quality, innovation, and financial sustainability: Central American entrepreneurial journalism through the lens of its audience. *Journalism Practice*, *12*(5), 543–564.

Harlow, S. (2021a). Entrepreneurial news sites as worthy causes? Exploring readers' motivations behind donating to Latin American journalism. *Digital Journalism*, *9*(3), 364–383.

Harlow, S. (2021b). A new people's press? Understanding digital-native news sites in Latin America as alternative media. *Digital Journalism*, 1–20. doi:10.1080/21670811.2021.1907204

Harlow, S. (2021c). Protecting news companies and their readers: Exploring social media policies in Latin American newsrooms. *Digital Journalism*, *9*(2), 176–195.

Harlow, S. & Chadha, M. (2019). Indian entrepreneurial journalism: Building a typology of how founders' social identity shapes innovation and sustainability. *Journalism Studies*, *20*(6), 891–910.

Harlow, S. & Harp, D. (2013). Alternative media in a digital era: Comparing news and information use among activists in the United States and Latin America. *Communication & Society*, *26*(4), 25–51.

Harlow, S. & Kilgo, D.K. (2021). Protest news and Facebook engagement: How the hierarchy of social struggle is rebuilt on social media. *Journalism & Mass Communication Quarterly*, *98*(3), 665–691.

Harlow, S., Kilgo, D.K., Salaverría, R., & García-Perdomo, V. (2020). Is the whole world watching? Building a typology of protest coverage on social media from around the world. *Journalism Studies*, *21*(11), 1590–1608.

Harlow, S., Salaverría, R., Kilgo, D.K., & García-Perdomo, V. (2017). Protest paradigm in multimedia: Social media sharing of coverage about the crime of Ayotzinapa, Mexico. *Journal of Communication*, *67*(3), 328–349.

Harlow, S. & Salaverría, R. (2016). Regenerating journalism: Exploring the 'alternativeness' and 'digital-ness' of online-native media in Latin America. *Digital Journalism*, *4*(8), 1001–1019.

Harp, D. (2007). *Desperately seeking women readers: US newspapers and the construction of a female readership*. Lexington Books.

Heiss, R., Schmuck, D., & Matthes, J. (2019). What drives interaction in political actors' Facebook posts? Profile and content predictors of user engagement and political actors' reactions. *Information, Communication & Society*, *22*(10), 1497–1513.

Hepp, A. & Loosen, W. (2021). Pioneer journalism: Conceptualizing the role of pioneer journalists and pioneer communities in the organizational refiguration of journalism. *Journalism*, *22*(3), 577–595.

Herscovitz, H. (2012). Brazilian journalists in the 21st century. In D. Weaver & L. Wilnat (Eds.), *The global journalist in the 21st Century* (pp. 365–381). New York, NY: Routledge.

Higgins Joyce, V.D.M. (2018). Independent voices of entrepreneurial news: Setting a new agenda in Latin America. *Palabra Clave*, *21*(3), 710–739.

Higgins Joyce, V.D.M. & Harlow, S. (2020). Seeking transnational, digital-native news from Latin America: An audience analysis through the lens of social capital. *Journalism Studies*, *21*(9), 1200–1219.

Higgins Joyce, V.D.M., Saldaña, M., Weiss, A.S., & Alves, R.C. (2017). Ethical perspectives in Latin America's journalism community: A comparative analysis of acceptance of controversial practice for investigative reporting. *International Communication Gazette*, *79*(5), 459–482.

Hirst, M. (2009). What is alternative journalism? *Global Media Journal*, *3*(1), 1–6.

Holt, K., Ustad Figenschou, T., & Frischlich, L. (2019). Key dimensions of alternative news media. *Digital Journalism*, *7*(7), 860–869.

Huesca, R. & Dervin, B. (1994). Theory and practice in Latin American alternative communication research. *Journal of Communication*, *44*(4), 53–73.

Hughes, S. & Lawson, C. (2005). The barriers to media opening in Latin America. *Political Communication*, *22*(1), 9–25.

IADB (2020). At least 77 million rural inhabitants have no access to high-quality internet services. Inter-American Development Bank. Available at: https://www.iadb.org/en/news/least-77-million-rural-inhabitants-have-no-access-high-quality-internet-services

Internet World Stats. (2021). Internet usage statistics for all the Americas. Available at https://www.internetworldstats.com/stats2.htm

Kilgo, D.K., Harlow, S., García-Perdomo, V., & Salaverría, R. (2018). From #Ferguson to #Ayotzinapa: Analyzing differences in domestic and foreign protest news shared on social media. *Mass Communication and Society*, *21*(5), 606–630.

Knight Center. (2013). Independent news sites in Latin America form new association. Knight Center for Journalism in the Americas, 20 June. Accessed 20 January 2016. https://knightcenter.utexas.edu/blog/00-14069-independent-news-sites-latin-america-form-new-association

Kollmann, T., Stöckmann, C., Hensellek, S., & Kensbock, J. (2016). *European startup monitor 2016*. German Startup Association. Available at: https://deutschestartups.org/wp-content/uploads/2019/07/European-Startup-Monitor-2016.pdf

Konieczna, M., Hatcher, J.A., & Moore, J.E. (2018). Citizen-centered journalism and contested boundaries: Innovations and limitations at three news organizations. *Journalism Practice*, *12*(1), 4–18.

Kossman, M. & Walsh, H. (2020). Latin America: Indigenous community reporters on joining forces and the COVID-19 crisis. *Deutsche Welle*. Available at: https://www.dw.com/en/latin-america-indigenouscommunity-reporterson-joining-forcesand-the-covid-19-crisis/a-54396548

Kuiken, J., Schuth, A., Spitters, M., & Marx, M. (2017). Effective headlines of newspaper articles in a digital environment. *Digital Journalism*, *5*(10), 1300–1314.

Laclau, E. & Mouffe, C. (1985). *Hegemony and socialist strategy: To a radical democratic politics* (W. Moore & P. Cammack, Trans.). London, UK: Verso.

Lasorsa, D.L., Lewis, S.C., & Holton, A.E. (2012). Normalizing Twitter: Journalism practice in an emerging communication space. *Journalism Studies*, *13*(1), 19–36.

References

Lee, A.M., Lewis, S.C., & Powers, M. (2014). Audience clicks and news placement: A study of time-lagged influence in online journalism. *Communication Research, 41*(4), 505–530.

Le Masurier, M. (2015). What is slow journalism? *Journalism Practice, 9*(2), 138–152.

Leung, D.K.K. & Lee, F.L.F. (2014). Cultivating an active online counterpublic: Examining usage and political impact of Internet alternative media. *The International Journal of Press/Politics, 19*, 340–359.

López, L. (2021, April 10). El Bus TV: el periodismo en Venezuela que vence la censura. *Gatopardo*. Available at: https://gatopardo.com/reportajes/el-bus-tv-el-periodismo-en-venezuela-que-vence-la-censura/

Lubianco, J. (2021). Racial and ethnic diversity in journalism: Greater representation attracts more readers, say speakers at Knight Center conference. *Knight Center for Journalism in the Americas*. Available at: https://knightcenter.utexas.edu/racial-and-ethnic-diversity-in-journalism-greater-representation-attracts-more-readers-say-speakers-at-knight-center-conference/

Marcus, G.E. (1994). On ideologies of reflexivity in contemporary efforts to remake the human sciences. *Poetics Today, 15*, 383–404.

Martín-Barbero, J. (1993). *Communication, culture and hegemony: From the media to mediations*. London: Sage.

Martínez, C. (2021). El oficio de estar en la escalera. *El Faro*. Available at https://elfaro.net/es/202111/columnas/25855/El-oficio-de-estar-en-la-escalera.htm

Martínez, M.P. (2018). Latino/a gender mobilizations in times of social media. *Journalism & Communication Monographs, 20*(2), 161–165.

Maslin, S.E. (2016). A light in the underworld. *Columbia Journalism Review*. Available at https://www.cjr.org/special_report/el_faro_el_salvador.php

McBride, K. (2021). New NPR ethics policy: It's OK for journalists to demonstrate (sometimes). *NPR*. Available at: https://www.npr.org/sections/publiceditor/2021/07/29/1021802098/new-npr-ethics-policy-its-ok-for-journalists-to-demonstrate-sometimes

McLeod, D.M. & Hertog, J.K. (1999). Social control, social change and the mass media's role in the regulation of protest groups. In D. Demers & K. Viswanath (Eds.), *Mass media, social control and social change: A macrosocial perspective* (pp. 305–332). Ames, IA: Iowa State University Press.

Meléndez Yúdico, J. (2016). Primer Estudio de Medios Digitales y Periodismo en América Latina: Iniciativas, Modelos de Negocio y Buenas Prácticas. *Mexico: Factual*. Available at https://drive.google.com/file/d/0B56C_0nwzk1HSHpsMUZpb0tQamM/view

Mellado, C., Humanes, M.L., & Márquez-Ramírez, M. (2018). The influence of journalistic role performance on objective reporting: A comparative study of Chilean, Mexican, and Spanish news. *International Communication Gazette, 80*(3), 250–272.

Mellado C., Márquez-Ramírez M., Mick J., Oller Alonso, M., & Olivera, D. (2017). Journalistic performance in Latin America: A comparative study of professional roles in news content. *Journalism, 18*(9), 1087–1106.

References

Mellado, C., Moreira, S.V., Lagos, C., et al. (2012). Comparing journalism cultures in Latin America: The case of Chile, Brazil and Mexico. *International Communication Gazette*, *74*(1), 60–77.

Méndez, M.C., Codina, L., & Salaverría, R. (2019). Qué son y qué no son los nuevos medios. 70 visiones de expertos hispanos. *Revista Latina de Comunicación Social*, *74*, 1506–1520.

Mesquita, L. & Fernandes, K. (2021). The new praxeology of digital journalism in Latin America: Media organizations learn how to walk by running. In *Journalism, Data and Technology in Latin America* (pp. 23–53). Palgrave Macmillan.

Mitchelstein, E., Matassi, M., & Boczkowski, P.J. (2020). Minimal effects, maximum panic: Social media and democracy in Latin America. *Social Media+ Society*, *6*(4), 2056305120984452

Molyneux, L., Holton, A., & Lewis, S.C. (2018). How journalists engage in branding on Twitter: Individual, organizational, and institutional levels. *Information, Communication & Society*, *21*(10), 1386–1401.

Mourão, R.R., & Harlow, S. (2020). Awareness, reporting, and branding: Exploring influences on Brazilian journalists' social media use across platforms. *Journal of Broadcasting & Electronic Media*, *64*(2), 215–235.

Mowbray, M. (2015). Alternative logics? Parsing the literature on alternative media. In *The Routledge Companion to Alternative and Community Media* (pp. 39–49). Routledge.

North, L. (2016). The gender of "soft" and "hard" news: Female journalists' views on gendered story allocations. *Journalism Studies*, *17*(3), 356–373.

OjoPúblico (2020). Chequeos en lenguas: una iniciativa de verificación sobre el Covid-19 para pueblos indígenas. Available at: https://ojo-publico.com/1776/ojopublico-inicia-chequeos-del-covid-19-en-lenguas-indigenas

Pavlik, J. (2013). Innovation and the future of journalism. *Digital Journalism*, *1*(2), 181–193.

Peterson-Salahuddin, C. (2021). Opening the gates: Defining a model of intersectional journalism. *Critical Studies in Media Communication*, *38*(5), 391–407.

Piqué, A.M. (2021). Carlos Dada: 'Nayib Bukele ha desmantelado la democracia en El Salvador.' *El Nacional*. Available at: https://www.elnacional.cat/es/internacional/entrevista-carlos-dada-nayib-bukele-desmantela-democracia-el-salvador_652112_102.html

Platon, S. & Deuze, M. (2003). Indymedia journalism: A radical way of making, selecting and sharing news? *Journalism*, *4*(3), 336–355.

Powers, E. & Yaros, R. (2012). Cultivating support for nonprofit news organizations: Commitment, trust and donating audiences. *Journal of Communication Management*, *17*(2), 157–170.

Rauch, J. (2015). Exploring the alternative–mainstream dialectic: What "alternative media" means to a hybrid audience. *Communication, Culture & Critique*, *8*(1), 124–143.

Rauch, J. (2016). Are there still alternatives? Relationships between alternative media and mainstream media in a converged environment. *Sociology Compass*, *10*(9), 756–767.

Rauch, J. (2021). *Resisting the news: Engaged audiences, alternative media, and popular critique of journalism.* Routledge.

Relly, J.E., & González de Bustamante, C. (2014). Silencing Mexico: A study of influences on journalists in the Northern States. *International Journal of Press/Politics, 19*(1), 108–131.

Requejo-Alemán, J.L. & Lugo-Ocando, J. (2014). Assessing the sustainability of Latin American investigative non-profit journalism. *Journalism Studies, 15*(5), 522–532.

Reyes Matta, F. (1983). *Comunicación Alternativa y Búsquedas Democráticas.* Chile: ILET - Friedrich Ebert Stiftung.

Richardson, A.V. (2020). *Bearing witness while Black: African Americans, smartphones, and the new protest #Journalism.* USA: Oxford University Press.

Riordan, M.A. & Glikson, E. (2020). On the hazards of the technology age: how using emojis affects perceptions of leaders. *International Journal of Business Communication,* 2329488420971690. doi:10.1177/2329488420971690

Robinson, J.J., Grennan, K., & Schiffrin, A. (2015). Publishing for peanuts. *Innovation and the journalism startup.* Report commissioned by the Open Society Foundation's Program for Independent Journalism. International Media, Advocacy, and Communications. Retrieved from http://www.cima.ned.org/wp-content/uploads/2015/11/PublishingforPeanuts.pdf

Rockwell, R. (2017). Evolving media structures in Central America. *International Journal of Media & Cultural Politics, 13*(1–2), 57–73.

Rockwell, R. & Janus, N. (2010). *Media Power in Central America.* University of Illinois Press.

Rodríguez, C. (2017). Studying media at the margins: Learning from the field. In *Media Activism in the Digital Age* (pp. 49–61). Routledge.

Rogers, E. (1995). *Diffusion of innovations* (4th ed.). New York: The Free Press.

Rovai, R. (2018). *Um Novo Ecossistema Midiático.* Ciudad Autónoma de Buenos Aires: CLACSO.

RSF. (2021). World press freedom index. *Reporters without Borders.* Available at https://rsf.org/en/ranking

Rubin, H.J. & Rubin, I.S. (2005). *Qualitative interviewing: The art of hearing data* (2nd ed.). Thousand Oaks, CA: Sage.

Rucht, D. (2004). The quadruple 'A'. *New Media, Citizens and Social Movements, 25.*

Russell, A. (2007) Digital communication networks and the journalistic field: The 2005 French riots. *Critical Studies in Media Communication, 24*(4), 285–302.

Said-Hung, E., Serrano-Tellería, A., García-De-Torres, E., Calderín, M., Rost, A., Arcila-Calderón, C., ... & Sánchez-Badillo, J. (2014). Ibero-American online news managers' goals and handicaps in managing social media. *Television & New Media, 15*(6), 577–589.

Salaverría, R. (ed.) (2016). *Ciberperiodismo en Iberoamérica.* Madrid, España: Fundación Telefónica y Editorial Ariel.

Salaverría, R. (2019). Digital journalism: 25 years of research. Review article. *El profesional de la información (EPI), 28*(1), 1–27.

References

Salaverría, R., & Corzo, S.M. (2020). Digital native media in Central America: Reshaping the online news sphere. In *The Politics of Technology in Latin America (Volume 2)* (pp. 149–160). Routledge.

Salaverría R., de-Lima-Santos, M.F. (2021). Transformation of the news media industry in the Global South. In: R. Salaverría & M.F. de-Lima-Santos (eds.), *Journalism, Data and Technology in Latin America*. Palgrave Macmillan.

Saldaña, M., Higgins Joyce, V.D.M., Schmitz Weiss, A., & Alves, R.C. (2017). Sharing the stage: Analysis of social media adoption by Latin American journalists. *Journalism Practice, 11*(4), 396–416.

Sandoval-Garcia, C. (2008). The media in Costa Rica: Many media, scarce communication. In J. Lugo-Ocando (Ed.), *The Media in Latin America* (pp. 100–115). New York: Open University Press.

Schmitz Weiss, A. (2015). The digital and social media journalist: A comparative analysis of journalists in Argentina, Brazil, Colombia, Mexico, and Peru. *International Communication Gazette, 77*(1), 74–101.

Schmitz Weiss, A., de Macedo Higgins Joyce, V., Saldaña, M., & Alves, R.C. (2017). Latin American investigative journalism education: Learning practices, learning gaps. *Journalism & Mass Communication Educator, 72*(3), 334–348.

Schmitz Weiss, A., De Macedo Higgins Joyce, V., Harlow, S., & Calmon Alves, R. (2018). Innovación y sostenibilidad: una relación examinada en organizaciones periodísticas emprendedoras de América Latina. *Cuadernos.info, 42*, 87–100.

Schmitz Weiss, A., de Macedo Higgins Joyce, V., Harlow, S., & Alves, R.C. (2020). Defining journalism innovation in Latin America: Exploration into perceptions among educators, students, and journalists. *Journalism & Mass Communication Educator, 75*(4), 419–435.

Schumpeter, J. (1943). *Capitalism, socialism and democracy*. London: Routledge.

Scott, M., Bunce, M., & Wright, K. (2019). Foundation funding and the boundaries of journalism. *Journalism Studies, 20*(14), 2034–2052.

Segura, M.S., & Waisbord, S. (2016). *Media movements: Civil society and media policy reform in Latin America*. Zed Books Ltd.

SembraMedia. (2017). *Inflection point. Impact, threats, and sustainability*. Available at http://data.sembramedia.org/

Shane, S. & Venkataraman, S. (2000). The promise of entrepreneurship as a field of research. *The Academy of Management Review, 25*(1), 217–226.

Simpson Grinberg, M. (1986). Trends in alternative communication research in Latin America. In R. Atwood & E.G. McAnany (Eds.), *Communication & Latin American Society: Trends in Critical Research, 1960–1985* (pp. 165–189). Madison, WI: University of Wisconsin Press.

Statista. (2020). Gross national income per capita in Latin America and the Caribbean in 2020, by country. Available at: https://www.statista.com/statistics/1066610/gross-national-income-per-capita-latin-america-caribbean/

Storsul, T. & Krumsvik, A.H. (2013). What is media innovation? In S. Storsul & A.H. Krumsvik (Eds.), *Media innovation: A multidisciplinary study of change* (pp. 13–26). Göteborg: Nordicom.

References

Suzina, A.C. (2021). *The evolution of popular communication in Latin America*. Cham: Palgrave Macmillan.

Tejedor, S., Ventín, A., Cervi, L., Pulido, C., & Tusa, F. (2020). Native media and business models: Comparative study of 14 successful experiences in Latin America. *Media and Communication, 8*(2), 146–158.

Tenenboim, O. & Cohen, A.A. (2015). What prompts users to click and comment: A longitudinal study of online news. *Journalism, 16*(2), 198–217.

Trilling, D., Tolochko, P., & Burscher, B. (2017). From newsworthiness to shareworthiness: How to predict news sharing based on article characteristics. *Journalism & Mass Communication Quarterly, 94*(1), 38–60.

Valentine, A., Kelly, M.L., Gringlas, S., & Doring, C. (2021). How newsroom leaders wrestled with covering a tumultuous year. *NPR*. https://www.npr.org/2021/06/03/1003020225/we-hold-these-truths-how-newsroom-leaders-wrestled-with-covering-a-tumultuous-ye

Valenzuela, S., Bachmann, I., & Bargsted, M. (2021). The personal is the political? What do Whatsapp users share and how it matters for news knowledge, polarization and participation in Chile. *Digital Journalism, 9*(2), 155–175.

Vinelli, N. (2014). *La televisión desde abajo. Historia, alternatividad y periodismo de contrainformación*. Buenos Aires: El Topo blindado/El río suena.

Vos, T.P., Craft, S., & Ashley, S. (2012). New media, old criticism: Bloggers' press criticism and the journalistic field. *Journalism, 13*(7), 850–868.

Waisbord, S. (2020). Mob censorship: Online harassment of US journalists in times of digital hate and populism. *Digital Journalism, 8*(8), 1030–1046.

Weaver, D.H. & Wilhoit, G.C. (1996). *The American journalist in the 1990s: U.S. News people at the end of an era*. Mahwah, NJ: Erlbaum.

Weinstein, M. (n.d.). Articulation theory for beginners. Available at www.personal.kent.edu/~mweinste/CI67095/Articulation.PDF

Welbers, K. & Opgenhaffen, M. (2019). Presenting news on social media: Media logic in the communication style of newspapers on Facebook. *Digital Journalism, 7*(1), 45–62.

Yezers'ka, L. & Zeta de Pozo, R. (2016). Perú. En: R. Salaverría (coord.). *Ciberperiodismo en Iberoamérica* (pp. 307–326). España: Fundación Telefónica y Editorial Ariel, S.A.

Zuluaga Trujillo, J. & Gómez Montero, S.M. (2019). Medios nativos digitales en América Latina: Agenda, sostenimiento e influencia. *Chasqui: Revista Latinoamericana de Comunicación*, (141), 301–316.

Index

active (alternative) audience, portrait of 89–103; "alternative" characteristics 98–100; audience characteristics 90–91; demographics 95–98; digital-native sites, advantages over mainstream media 91–95; mobilizing readers and protest participation 100–102
activism vs. journalism 9, 29, 56, 66–68, 81–85, 88, 118; in El Salvador 81–82; in Guatemala 82–84; journalism as 59–60, 69; in Mexico 84–85; that transforms 81–85
Agencia Ocote 80
Agência Pública 80
Aguirre, Laura 38, 57, 60, 62, 64–66, 68
Alanís, Francisco 17, 20, 38
Albarrán, Luis Miguel 84
Alharaca 38, 57, 62, 64–65, 68, 114
Aliados (Allies) network 5
alternative journalism 2, 6–7, 67, 84; amateurs 7; critique of mainstream 24, 75–76; fundamental tenets of 100; independence 27; liminal spaces of operation of 9, 88; mainstream vs. 25, 105, 107–108, 112, 117–118; in times of violence 33–34
alternative media 2, 86; amelioration role of sites in 8–9; audience engagement 89–103; characteristics of 72, 75, 79, 111; creativity 46; critique of mainstream 30, 80, 87; empowerment 28, 89; heterodox-creative logics of 36, 46, 49, 52–53; as innovating 23, 28, 30; mainstream vs. 73–74, 79, 88, 115; marginalization of 12; participatory ethos of 28; relational definition of 103; role of 89; sites as 5–6, 97, 102–103; traditional conceptions of 24; ways to refer to 7
Animal Político 18, 31, 76–77, 80, 84
Arce Teceros 56–58, 63–64, 69
Argentina 10, 97
articulation 107–115; actors 108; audiences 112–113; constraints 108; content 108; context 108; contingent 108; financing 109–110; identity 115; news values, practices, and content 111–112; norms and ideology 113–114; professionalism 110–111
Atton, C. 9, 107
audiences 112–113; *see also* active (alternative) audience, portrait of; characteristics 90–9; interaction in social media 50–53
Ávila, Jennifer 40, 43, 58, 61–64, 66–68, 70
Avilés, Marco 71

behaviors 36
Benson, R. 115
BN Periodismo 36, 45

Bolivia 10
bottom-up, community-centric approach 76–77
Bourdieu, P. 9, 105–106
Brazil 10, 80

Carpentier, N. 87
cause-based digital-native sites 13, 20, 55, 66, 114–115
Chávez, Hugo 47
Chequeos en Lenguas (Fact-checking in Languages) 71
Chicas Poderosas 56, 63
Chile 11, 47, 100
CIPER 45
citizen participation 7, 23, 27–28, 43, 52, 74–75, 77–79
Clave Digital 4
Clinic, The 45
Colombia 5, 10, 41, 47–48, 75, 77, 80, 94, 96, 100–101
community-centric approach 76–77, 108, 111
"conscientization" 72
content analysis 45–53
ContraCorriente 58, 61–64, 66–67
Costa Rica 100
country comparisons 47
crowdfunding 32
Cuba 11

Dada, Carlos 1–3, 44, 82, 104
de Leo, Juan Pablo 31
democracy 35, 86, 89, 95, 114–115, 119; alternative media and 79; citizens and 29, 111; community and 100; human rights and 103; journalism for, importance 80; as journalistic values 82; toward the left and radical social 47
Deuze, M. 9
dialogic communication 72
digital-native sites 79–82; *see also El Faro* (lighthouse); audiences 112–113; cause-based 13, 20, 55, 66, 114–115; centrality of violence to 33; editorial freedom among 27; in Guatemala 86; independence 5, 9; levels of 116; mainstream media and, advantages over 91–95; mainstream stories versus, in Mexico 26; mainstream versus, in social media 26; of Mexico 84; *OjoPúblico* 71–72; readers access 92–95, 96; readers preferred media traits 98, 99; readers protest participation 100, 101; rise in Latin America 1–16; social media helping 45; transnational audiences of 90
digital-native vs. mainstream 37–40, 39; content characteristics 43; journalists 38, 41–42
(dis)articulations 104–120; *see also* articulation
disruptions 115–117
Dominican Republic 4, 11
donation campaigns 32
Downing, J. 90
doxa 105

Ecuador 11, 47, 80
editorial independence 19–20, 23, 25, 111–112; at *Animal Político* 76; digital-native sites' 87; financial and 4–5, 13, 19–20, 22, 27, 29–30, 33, 89, 98, 104, 108, 110, 116
Efecto Cocuyo 45, 61–62, 67, 76
El Confidencial 77
El Faro 1–4, 24, 44–45, 76–77, 81–82, 104, 114; awards received 5; financial and editorial independence of 4–5, 13
El Pitazo 35, 37, 44–45
El Salvador 11, 26–27, 81–82, 84, 97, 100
emojis 49–50
entrepreneurial journalism/media 18; business models 20; in Mexico 19–20; opportunity 19–20; sustainability and innovation 20
ethnocentrism 14–16

Facebook 38
Falck, H.S. 36
feminist reporting norms 59–61; *see also* journalism with a feminist gaze
Festa, R. 7

field theory 105–107
financial independence 23–25, 27, 31, 33, 75, 97, 103
Flores-Márquez, D. 15
Forde, S. 24, 74–75, 79
Freedman, D. 7
Freire, P. 72
Fuchs, C. 73
funding for online journalism 23–24

García-Perdomo, V. 5
gender 80, 94–95, 117, 119; see also journalism with a feminist gaze; cause-based sites and 114; in predicting digital-native news sites' readers protest participation 101; in predicting journalists' social media use for work 41; in predicting readers access to digital-native news sites 96; role in digital-native media 13
GIFs 50
GK 59, 63, 65, 67, 69, 76, 80
Global Media Monitoring Project (GMMP) 58, 71
González, Isabel 55
González de Bustamante 18
Guatemala 11, 26–27, 80, 82–84

Hájek, R. 87
Hamilton, J.F. 9, 80, 107
Harcup, T. 7, 9, 25, 28, 73, 89–90
hashtags 49–50
Hepp, A. 21
Hernández, Lizbeth 17–18, 20, 31–32
heterodox-creative logics 46, 111
Holt, K. 74, 103
Honduras 11
human rights 28, 116–118; in Colombian outlets 47; digital-native sites' websites 80; digital-native startups' content and 25, 43; *El Faro* expressing 104, 114; El Salvador digital-native sites in 82, 86; feminist perspectives 55–56; journalists responsibility 59–63, 67; *La Nota*'s focus 55, 67; news sites focus on 58; through emojis and hashtags 49

Iberoamerica 4

identity 115; entrepreneurial identity 8, 19, 30; as independent and different than traditional media 4; Latin American sites 117–118; of Mexican journalists 33; *OjoPúblico's* 71; professional identity 78–79, 111; self-perceptions about 14
Indymedia 9
infographics 50
Instagram: content, comparison by country 47, 48; Instagram-specific story format 38; interactions in, predictors of 50, 51; tactics 46
internet 115; active audience through 91, 103; going against the current 29–30; in independent journalism 1–16, 37; news media system and 115; penetration in Latin America 37, 45

journalism; see also active (alternative) audience, portrait of; activism vs. 66, 81–85; alternative journalism/media 73–75; audience relationships 50–53, 89–103, 112–113; bottom-up, community-centric approach 76–77; citizen participation 77–78; content 111–112; critiquing the mainstream 75–76; ethics, norms and values 78; financing 23, 109–110; investigative journalism 75, 78, 86, 93, 113–114, 116; news values 23, 43, 50, 56–57, 105, 109, 111–112, 116, 118; objectivity 59–61, 80, 83, 85, 92, 113–114; professional identity 78–79; that reforms, transforms, generating 71–88; routines 78; social media for 37; sources 85–89; stance-taking and justice-driven journalism 79–81
journalism with a feminist gaze 55–70; business models 63–64; change agents 69–70; feminist media or feminist practices? 66–68; feminist reporting norms 59–61; filling an unmet need 57–59; contesting "macho media" hegemony 56–57; organizational

structures 63–64; safety and mental health 64–66; sourcing, reporting 61–63; transformed work culture 63–64
justice-driven journalism 79–81

Kaja Negra 31
Knight Center for Journalism in the Americas 12, 16

La Historia 76
La Nota 55, 67–68
La Oreja Roja 45, 50
La Silla Vacía 45, 50, 75, 80
Latin America, independent, digital-native sites rise in 1–16; *see also El Faro*; alternative journalism 6–7; mainstream, ameliorating 7–8; mainstream media, shortcomings of 7–8; at the margins 8–10, 104, 107–109, 111, 113–119
Latin American journalism 10–16; Argentina 10; Bolivia 10; Brazil 10; cause-based digital-native sites 13; Chile 11; Cuba 11; Dominican Republic 11; Ecuador 11; El Salvador 11; ethnocentrism 14–16; Guatemala 11; Honduras 11; Mexico 11; Nicaragua 11; Peru 11; Uruguay 11; Venezuela 11
Ledesma, Ernesto 31, 85
LGBTQ-plus communities 111
Loosen, W. 21

"macho media" hegemony, contesting 56–57
Magaña, M.I. 5
mainstream media: alternative journalism critique of 24–25, 75–76, 105, 107–108, 112, 117–118; alternative media critique of 30, 73–74, 79–80, 87–88, 115; ameliorating 7–8, 117–119; digital-native sites advantages over 91–95; digital-native vs., in content characteristics 37–40, 41–43; digital-native vs., in social media 26, 37–40; digital-native vs. online journalism in Mexico 26; journalism critiquing 75–76; shortcomings of 7–8
Mariona, Milagro 40, 44, 55, 59, 67–69
Martín-Barbero, J. 74
Mexico, online journalism in 11, 17–34, 80, 84–85, 97; against the current 29–30; *Animal Político* 18, 31, 33; content 25–27; *Crash* 33; digital-native versus mainstream stories 26; editorial independence 25; *El Faro* 24; entrepreneurial opportunity 19–20; funding 23–24; interventionism 29; *Kaja Negra* 17, 31, 33; participation, collaboration 27–28; *Pie de Página* 18, 31; *Plumas Atómicas* 33; *Político Mx* 31; *Sopitas* 17; sustainability and innovation 20–21; technology 21–23; violence as entrepreneurial opportunity 30–33
misogyny 67
mob censorship 65
Mowbray, M. 53
Mujeres Referentes database 61

Naveda, Enrique 83, 85
Nicaragua 4, 11, 97, 100
non-normative behaviors 36
normative behaviors 36

objectivity 59–61, 80, 83, 85, 92, 113–114
OjoPúblico 71–72, 80
Open Society Foundation (OSF) 19

Pastrana, Daniela 18, 27, 31–32, 84
patriarchal hegemony 56
Pavlik, J. 19
Peru 11, 80
Pie de Página 18, 31
Platon, S. 9
Plaza Pública 83
Político Mx 31
Primicias 45, 80
professional identity 78–79
professionalism 110–111
protests 11, 26, 32, 47, 90–91, 100–102, 113, 117

Rauch, J. 7
Relly, J.E. 18
Reyes, Luz Mely 61, 64, 67, 69
rhetorical creativity 46
Riera, Carmen 45, 61, 63, 65–66
Rodríguez, C. 73
Rogers, E. 19
Rucht, D. 7

Salaverría, R. 5, 12, 16n1
Sandoval, M. 73
Sanz, Jose Luís 45
Segura, M.S. 11–12
SembraMedia 30
sexism 67
Sexo Sinvergüenzas 57
Simán, Jorge 1
social media 35–53; audience interaction 50–53; behaviors to adopt 36; branding 40; content analysis 45–53; country comparisons 47; digital-native vs. mainstream 37–40; emojis 49–50; for journalism 37; GIFs 50; hashtags 49–50; heterodox-creative logic 46; infographics 50; likes, comments, action! 35–53; limitations 44–45; monitoring the news 40, 44; reporting 40, 43; traditional media's normalization of 36
social change 13–14, 19, 34, 74, 81–82, 87
social justice 46, 49–50, 52, 81, 94
social movements 25, 28–29, 46, 57–58, 73, 90
Sopitas 17, 38
Suzina, A.C. 74–75, 79

Twitter 38, 106

Uruguay 11

Vallejo, Mael 18, 31
Venezuela 10–11, 23–24, 28, 30, 35, 44–45, 47–48, 51, 61, 76, 78
Vos, T.P. 106

Waisbord, S. 11–12, 65

Taylor & Francis eBooks

www.taylorfrancis.com

A single destination for eBooks from Taylor & Francis with increased functionality and an improved user experience to meet the needs of our customers.

90,000+ eBooks of award-winning academic content in Humanities, Social Science, Science, Technology, Engineering, and Medical written by a global network of editors and authors.

TAYLOR & FRANCIS EBOOKS OFFERS:

- A streamlined experience for our library customers
- A single point of discovery for all of our eBook content
- Improved search and discovery of content at both book and chapter level

REQUEST A FREE TRIAL
support@taylorfrancis.com

For Product Safety Concerns and Information please contact our EU representative GPSR@taylorandfrancis.com
Taylor & Francis Verlag GmbH, Kaufingerstraße 24, 80331 München, Germany

www.ingramcontent.com/pod-product-compliance
Lightning Source LLC
Chambersburg PA
CBHW051750230426
43670CB00012B/2223